# Amazing Weekly Workouts for Year 6!

This CGP book is bursting with speedy 10-Minute Workouts that are great for warm-ups, recaps, homework and more.

Each Workout is focused on building pupils' Arithmetic skills with more challenging questions introduced throughout the book. By the end of Year 6, there'll be no stopping them!

We've even included cut-out-and-keep answers, plus a useful progress chart to keep track of their marks.

# How to Use this Book

- This book contains 36 workouts. We've split them into 3 sections — one for each term, with 12 workouts each. There's roughly one workout for every week of the school year.

- Each workout is out of 16 marks and should take about 10 minutes.

- Each workout starts with some Quick Fire questions, which are a perfect warm-up before the main questions.

- The first 3 workouts only contain Year 5 Arithmetic content — they're ideal for reminding pupils what they learnt in the previous year. These workouts should be done at the start of Year 6.

- The final 12 workouts cover all of the Year 6 Arithmetic content — they're a great way to recap the year, and ensure that pupils have got to grips with the Year 6 topics.

- New topics are gradually introduced, and then re-tested throughout the later workouts. The workouts increase in difficulty as you progress.

- The contents pages show you where each Arithmetic topic is first introduced.

- The tick boxes on the contents pages can help you to keep a record of which workouts have been attempted.

- A Puzzle page, cut-out Answers and a Progress Chart can be found at the back of the book.

---

Published by CGP
ISBN: 978 1 78908 471 9

Editors: Adam Bartlett, Sean McParland,
Caley Simpson, Ben Train

With thanks to Amanda MacNaughton and
Glenn Rogers for the proofreading.

With thanks to Lottie Edwards
for the copyright research.

Clipart from Corel®

Contains public sector information licensed under the Open Government Licence v3.0 http://www.nationalarchives.gov.uk/doc/open-government-licence/version/3/

Printed by Bell and Bain Ltd, Glasgow.

Based on the classic CGP style created by Richard Parsons.

Text, design, layout and original illustrations
© Coordination Group Publications Ltd. (CGP) 2020
All rights reserved.

Photocopying this book is not permitted, even if you have a CLA licence.
Extra copies are available from CGP with next day delivery • 0800 1712 712 • www.cgpbooks.co.uk

# Contents — Autumn Term

- [x] **Workout 1** .................................................................................................................. 2
  - Recap of Year 5 material.

- [x] **Workout 2** .................................................................................................................. 4
  - Recap of Year 5 material.

- [x] **Workout 3** .................................................................................................................. 6
  - Recap of Year 5 material.

- [x] **Workout 4** .................................................................................................................. 8
  - Order and compare numbers up to 10 000 000.
  - Multiply and divide numbers by 10, 100 and 1000, giving answers with up to three decimal places.

- [x] **Workout 5** ................................................................................................................ 10
  - Round any whole number to a required degree of accuracy.
  - Use negative numbers and calculate intervals across 0.

- [x] **Workout 6** ................................................................................................................ 12
  - Divide a 3-digit number by a 2-digit number using short division, without any remainders.
  - Perform mental calculations with mixed operations.

- [x] **Workout 7** ................................................................................................................ 14
  - Use the order of operations to carry out calculations involving the four operations.

- [x] **Workout 8** ................................................................................................................ 16
  - Divide a 4-digit number by a 2-digit number using short division, without any remainders.
  - Perform mental calculations with large numbers.

- [x] **Workout 9** ................................................................................................................ 18
  - Multiply a 4-digit number by a 2-digit number using long multiplication.

- [x] **Workout 10** .............................................................................................................. 20
  - Use common factors to simplify fractions.
  - Divide a 3-digit number by a 2-digit number using short division, with remainders.

- [x] **Workout 11** .............................................................................................................. 22
  - Use common multiples to express fractions with the same denominator.

- [x] **Workout 12** .............................................................................................................. 24
  - Divide a 4-digit number by a 2-digit number using short division, with remainders.
  - Compare and order fractions, including fractions greater than 1.

# Contents — Spring Term

☑ **Workout 1** .................................................................................................... **26**
  • Add and subtract fractions with different denominators using equivalent fractions.

☑ **Workout 2** .................................................................................................... **28**
  • Divide a 3-digit number by a 2-digit number using long division, without any remainders.

☑ **Workout 3** .................................................................................................... **30**
  • Add and subtract fractions and mixed numbers with different denominators using equivalent fractions.
  • Multiply 1-digit numbers with one decimal place by whole numbers.

☑ **Workout 4** .................................................................................................... **32**
  • Divide a 4-digit number by a 2-digit number using long division, without any remainders.

☑ **Workout 5** .................................................................................................... **34**
  • Multiply simple pairs of proper fractions.
  • Multiply 1-digit numbers with two decimal places by whole numbers.

☑ **Workout 6** .................................................................................................... **36**
  • Divide a 3-digit number by a 2-digit number using long division, with remainders.

☑ **Workout 7** .................................................................................................... **38**
  • Divide proper fractions by whole numbers.

☑ **Workout 8** .................................................................................................... **40**
  • Use division to calculate decimal fraction equivalents for a simple fraction.

☑ **Workout 9** .................................................................................................... **42**
  • Use written division methods in cases where the answer has one decimal place.

☑ **Workout 10** .................................................................................................. **44**
  • Divide a 4-digit number by a 2-digit number using long division, with remainders.
  • Use written division methods in cases where the answer has two decimal places.

☑ **Workout 11** .................................................................................................. **46**
  • Use equivalences between simple fractions, decimals and percentages.

☑ **Workout 12** .................................................................................................. **48**
  • Calculate percentages of amounts.

# Contents — Summer Term

- [x] **Workout 1** .................................................................. 50
  - Recap of Year 6 material.
- [x] **Workout 2** .................................................................. 52
  - Recap of Year 6 material.
- [x] **Workout 3** .................................................................. 54
  - Recap of Year 6 material.
- [x] **Workout 4** .................................................................. 56
  - Recap of Year 6 material.
- [x] **Workout 5** .................................................................. 58
  - Recap of Year 6 material.
- [x] **Workout 6** .................................................................. 60
  - Recap of Year 6 material.
- [x] **Workout 7** .................................................................. 62
  - Recap of Year 6 material.
- [x] **Workout 8** .................................................................. 64
  - Recap of Year 6 material.
- [x] **Workout 9** .................................................................. 66
  - Recap of Year 6 material.
- [x] **Workout 10** ................................................................ 68
  - Recap of Year 6 material.
- [x] **Workout 11** ................................................................ 70
  - Recap of Year 6 material.
- [x] **Workout 12** ................................................................ 72
  - Recap of Year 6 material.
- [x] **Puzzle** ....................................................................... 74
- **Answers** ..................................................................... 75

# Autumn Term: Workout 1

**Quick Fire**

Try to work out the answers to these in your head.

1.  a) 6812 + 4000 = ............     b) 3446 + 5100 = ............

    c) 8063 − 2000 = ............     d) 7521 − 3300 = ............

    *2 marks*

2.  a) 54 ÷ 10 = ............     b) 12.3 × 10 = ............

    c) 4.9 × 10 = ............     d) 7.1 ÷ 10 = ............

    *2 marks*

**Now try these:**

3.  What is 459 637 rounded to the nearest:

    a) 10 000? ............................

    b) 100 000? ............................

    *2 marks*

4.  Write the decimals below as fractions.

    a) $0.9 = \dfrac{\square}{\square}$     b) $0.53 = \dfrac{\square}{\square}$

    *2 marks*

5. Count **backwards** in steps of 10 000 to fill in the blanks.

   183 657   ....................   ....................   ....................

   2 marks

6. Work out:

   a) $5^2$ = ..............

   b) $7^2$ = ..............

   2 marks

7. Fill in the boxes with **>** or **<** to make the sentences true.

   a) 775 445 ☐ 775 384

   b) 348 761 ☐ 384 671

   2 marks

8. Work out:

   a) 156 023 + 435 782

   b) 367 119 + 41 543

   2 marks

How did you do?

Score:

Autumn Term: Workout 1

# Autumn Term: Workout 2

**Quick Fire**

Try to work out the answers to these in your head.

1. a) 16 842 + 20 000 = ..................

   b) 2891 + 34 000 = ..................

   c) 57 063 − 30 000 = ..................

   d) 22 054 − 11 000 = ..................

   *2 marks*

2. a) 38 ÷ 100 = ............   b) 95 ÷ 100 = ............

   c) 1.55 × 100 = ............   d) 0.37 × 100 = ............

   *2 marks*

## Now try these:

3. Fill in the boxes with > or < to make the sentences true.

   a) $\frac{4}{8}$ ☐ $\frac{9}{16}$   b) $\frac{24}{35}$ ☐ $\frac{5}{7}$

   *2 marks*

4. Work out:

   a) $2^3$ = ............   b) $4^3$ = ............

   *2 marks*

5. Write the improper fractions below as mixed numbers.

   a) $\frac{14}{5} =$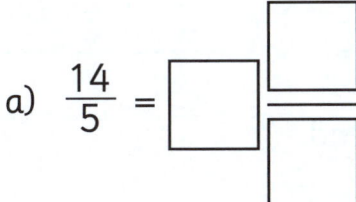
   
   b) $\frac{27}{8} =$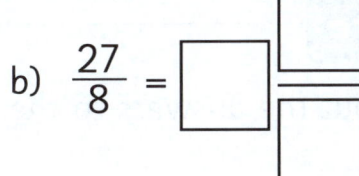

   *2 marks*

6. Work out:

   a) 384.617 − 193.546
   
   b) 727.183 − 35.243

   *2 marks*

7. Write the fractions below as decimals.

   a) $\frac{4}{5} =$ ..............
   
   b) $\frac{14}{25} =$ ..............

   *2 marks*

8. Work out:

   a) 264 × 35
   
   b) 367 × 42

   *2 marks*

How did you do?

Score:

# Autumn Term: Workout 3

## Quick Fire

Try to work out the answers to these in your head.

1. a) 29 × 5 = ..............  b) 14 × 50 = ..............

   c) 168 ÷ 8 = ..............  d) 500 ÷ 25 = ..............

   *2 marks*

2. a) 0.84 × 1000 = ..............  b) 4.5 × 1000 = ..............

   c) 7700 ÷ 1000 = ..............  d) 160 ÷ 1000 = ..............

   *2 marks*

## Now try these:

3. Count **backwards** in steps of 20 to fill in the blanks.

   34    14    ..............    ..............    ..............

   *2 marks*

4. What is 67% as:

   a) a fraction?  ☐/100

   b) a decimal?  ..............

   *2 marks*

5. Round:

   a) 4.54 to the nearest whole number  ..................

   b) 8.73 to one decimal place  ..................

   *2 marks*

6. Work out the sums below. Write your answers as mixed numbers.

   a) $\frac{2}{3} + \frac{11}{12} = \square\frac{\square}{\square}$   b) $\frac{3}{4} + \frac{7}{8} = \square\frac{\square}{\square}$

   *2 marks*

7. Put the numbers below in order from **smallest** to **largest**.

   4.35    4.358    4.4    4.341

   .......... .......... .......... ..........
   smallest                          largest

   *2 marks*

8. Work out:

   a) 7 ) 5 3 2    b) 8 ) 1 0 9 6

   *2 marks*

How did you do?                    Score:

# Autumn Term: Workout 4

## Quick Fire

Try to work out the answers to these in your head.

1.  a) 7724 − 4200 = ............    b) 4915 + 2400 = ............

    c) 6158 − 3500 = ............    d) 2726 + 6300 = ............

    *2 marks*

2.  a) 51 × 8 = ............    b) 15 × 20 = ............

    c) 636 ÷ 6 = ............    d) 800 ÷ 16 = ............

    *2 marks*

## Now try these:

3.  Put the numbers below in order from **largest** to **smallest**.

    3 684 219    3 716 441    3 687 045    3 684 228

    .................   .................   .................   .................
    largest                                                     smallest

    *2 marks*

4.  Work out:

    a) 5.601 × 100 = ............    b) 19.2 ÷ 100 = ............

    c) 0.284 × 1000 = ............   d) 35 ÷ 1000 = ............

    *4 marks*

5. Work out:

   a) 279.36 + 57.268

   b) 378.059 + 582.93

   *2 marks*

6. Work out the products below.
   Write your answers as mixed numbers.

   a) $\frac{7}{10} \times 3 =$ ☐ $\frac{☐}{☐}$

   b) $2\frac{4}{5} \times 4 =$ ☐ $\frac{☐}{☐}$

   *2 marks*

7. Work out:

   a) 6 ) 8 2 2

   b) 7 ) 4 7 0 4

   *2 marks*

How did you do?

Score: ☐

# Autumn Term: Workout 5

## Quick Fire

Try to work out the answers to these in your head.

1. a) 42 ÷ 10 = ............   b) 0.23 × 10 = ............

   c) 75 ÷ 100 = ............   d) 8.1 × 100 = ............

   *2 marks*

2. a) 99 × 7 = ............   b) 51 × 5 = ............

   c) 909 ÷ 9 = ............   d) 8004 ÷ 4 = ............

   *2 marks*

## Now try these:

3. Round:

   a) 6 274 688 to the nearest million   ............................

   b) 3 519 939 to the nearest thousand   ............................

   *2 marks*

4. Work out:

   a) 5 − 8 = ............   b) −7 + 9 = ............

   c) −10 + 15 = ............   d) 17 − 11 = ............

   *4 marks*

5. Put the numbers below in order from **smallest** to **largest**.

   7 327 910      6 727 154      7 346 804      7 346 637

   .................  .................  .................  .................
   smallest                                        largest

   2 marks

6. Write the fractions below as decimals.

   a) $\frac{2}{5}$ = ..............

   b) $\frac{11}{20}$ = ..............

   2 marks

7. Work out:

   a) 5716 × 6                b) 2739 × 3

   2 marks

How did you do?               Score:

# Autumn Term: Workout 6

**Quick Fire**

Try to work out the answers to these in your head.

1. a) 5847 − .............. = 5441
   b) 6280 + .............. = 6483
   c) .............. + 541 = 6841
   d) .............. − 202 = 1658

   *2 marks*

2. a) 1.72 × 10 = ..............
   b) 2.4 ÷ 100 = ..............
   c) 186 ÷ 1000 = ..............
   d) 5.117 × 100 = ..............

   *2 marks*

**Now try these:**

3. Work out:

   a) 11 ⟌ 3 9 6
   b) 15 ⟌ 6 4 5

   *2 marks*

4. Work out the calculations below in your head.

   a) 15 + 10 − 8 = ..............
   b) 25 − 14 + 11 = ..............
   c) 4 × 8 ÷ 2 = ..............
   d) 42 ÷ 7 × 9 = ..............

   *4 marks*

5. Work out:

   a) 425.54 + 390.451

   b) 823.288 − 170.23

2 marks

6. Work out the sums below.
   Write your answers as mixed numbers.

   a) $\frac{4}{5} + \frac{6}{25}$ = ☐ $\frac{☐}{☐}$

   b) $\frac{13}{18} + \frac{2}{3}$ = ☐ $\frac{☐}{☐}$

2 marks

7. Work out:

   a) 3576 ÷ 12

   b) 2979 ÷ 9

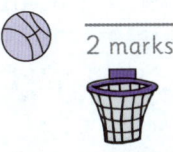

2 marks

How did you do?

Score:

# Autumn Term: Workout 7

## Quick Fire

Try to work out the answers to these in your head.

1.  a) 6.078 × 100 = ............    b) 0.81 × 1000 = ............

    c) 3007 ÷ 1000 = ............    d) 6.1 ÷ 100 = ............

    *2 marks*

2.  a) 44 × 5 = ............    b) 101 × 12 = ............

    c) 424 ÷ 4 = ............    d) 816 ÷ 8 = ............

    *2 marks*

## Now try these:

3.  Work out:

    a) 24 ÷ (9 − 3) = ............    b) 16 + 5 × 12 = ............

    *2 marks*

4.  Fill in the boxes with **>** or **<** to make the sentences true.

    a) 2 957 349 ☐ 2 961 327

    b) 8 818 613 ☐ 8 781 944

    *2 marks*

5. What is 51% as:

   a) a fraction? $\frac{\Box}{100}$     b) a decimal? ..............

   *2 marks*

6. What is 5 308 943 rounded to the nearest:

   a) 10 000? ..............................

   b) 1 000 000? ..............................

   *2 marks*

7. Work out:

   a) $\frac{5}{6} - \frac{19}{36} = \frac{\Box}{\Box}$     b) $\frac{21}{32} - \frac{3}{8} = \frac{\Box}{\Box}$

   *2 marks*

8. Work out:

   a) (7 + 33) ÷ 4 = ............     b) 20 − 10 × 3 = ............

   *2 marks*

How did you do?    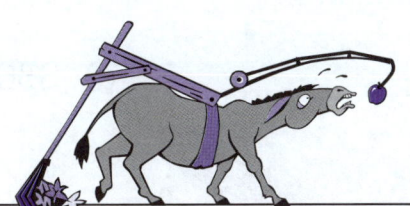    Score:

# Autumn Term: Workout 8

## Quick Fire

Try to work out the answers to these in your head.

1.  a) 21 078 + 51 000 = ..................

    b) 8482 + 64 000 = ..................

    c) 80 337 − 35 000 = ..................

    d) 26 194 − 23 000 = ..................

    *2 marks*

2.  a) 49 ÷ 1000 = ..............     b) 7.5 ÷ 100 = ..............

    c) 0.062 × 1000 = ..............     d) 5.441 × 100 = ..............

    *2 marks*

## Now try these:

3.  Work out:

    a) 12 ) 2 4 3 6     b) 11 ) 6 6 3 3

    *2 marks*

4.  Work out the calculations below in your head.

    a) 600 × 5 = ..............     b) 120 × 40 = ..............

    c) 4200 ÷ 7 = ..............     d) 3300 ÷ 110 = ..............

    *4 marks*

5. Work out:

   a) 15 − 19 = ..............

   b) −13 + 16 = ..............

2 marks

6. Work out:

   a) 647 × 37

   b) 865 × 31

2 marks

7. Work out:

   a) 12 ) 4 9 3 2

   b) 13 ) 2 7 6 9

2 marks

How did you do?

Score:

# Autumn Term: Workout 9

## Quick Fire

Try to work out the answers to these in your head.

1.  a) 16 − 12 + 13 = ............   b) 34 + 18 − 22 = ............

    c) 8 × 7 ÷ 2 = ............   d) 72 ÷ 12 × 11 = ............
    
    *2 marks*

2.  a) 2.101 × 1000 = ............   b) 0.093 × 10 = ............

    c) 3.7 ÷ 100 = ............   d) 188 ÷ 1000 = ............
    
    *2 marks*

## Now try these:

3.  Work out:

    a) 2092 × 24   b) 1263 × 71

    *2 marks*

4.  Write the fractions below as percentages.

    a) $\frac{39}{50}$ = ............ %   b) $\frac{7}{20}$ = ............ %
    
    *2 marks*

5. Round:

   a) 7.39 to the nearest whole number ......................

   b) 4.27 to one decimal place ......................

   2 marks

6. Work out:

   a) $\dfrac{2}{7} + \dfrac{13}{21} = \dfrac{\Box}{\Box}$
   
   b) $\dfrac{23}{36} - \dfrac{4}{9} = \dfrac{\Box}{\Box}$

   2 marks

7. Work out the multiplications below.
   Write your answers as mixed numbers.

   a) $\dfrac{5}{8} \times 5 = \Box\dfrac{\Box}{\Box}$
   
   b) $3\dfrac{2}{5} \times 3 = \Box\dfrac{\Box}{\Box}$

   2 marks

8. Work out:

   a) 255 ÷ 15
   
   b) 2664 ÷ 18

   2 marks

How did you do?

Score:

Autumn Term: Workout 9

# Autumn Term: Workout 10

## Quick Fire

Try to work out the answers to these in your head.

1.  a) 8 − 13 = ............   b) −11 + 16 = ............

    c) 25 − 42 = ............  d) −17 + 35 = ............

    *2 marks*

2.  Write the fractions below in their simplest form.

    a) $\frac{6}{9} = \frac{\Box}{\Box}$   b) $\frac{18}{24} = \frac{\Box}{\Box}$

    *2 marks*

## Now try these:

3.  Tick the true number sentences below.

    $\frac{16}{15} = \frac{4}{5}$ ☐     $\frac{21}{28} = \frac{3}{4}$ ☐

    $\frac{20}{32} = \frac{5}{8}$ ☐     $\frac{35}{48} = \frac{5}{6}$ ☐

    *2 marks*

4.  Work out:

    a) 12 ⟌ 5 2 1    r ____

    b) 11 ⟌ 6 9 7    r ____

    *2 marks*

5.  Work out:

    a) 975 654 + 53 351

    b) 641.696 + 65.385

    *2 marks*

6.  Work out:

    a) 4 × (8 − 3) = ...............

    b) 2 + 8 ÷ 4 = ...............

    c) 28 ÷ (7 × 2) = ...............

    d) 35 − 25 ÷ 5 = ...............

    *4 marks*

7.  Work out:

    a) 532 216 − 38 026

    b) 479.84 − 209.925

    *2 marks*

**How did you do?**

**Score:**

# Autumn Term: Workout 11

**Quick Fire**

Try to work out the answers to these in your head.

1. a) $30 \times 800 =$ ............    b) $3200 \div 80 =$ ............

   c) $54\,000 \div 90 =$ ............    d) $12 \times 800 =$ ............

   *2 marks*

2. a) $3.85 \times 1000 =$ ............    b) $0.72 \div 10 =$ ............

   c) $8.994 \times 100 =$ ............    d) $62.6 \div 100 =$ ............

   *2 marks*

**Now try these:**

3. Fill in the boxes below to make each fraction equivalent to $\frac{5}{6}$.

   a) $\dfrac{\Box}{18}$        b) $\dfrac{30}{\Box}$

   *2 marks*

4. Fill in the boxes with > or < to make the sentences true.

   a) $\frac{5}{7}\ \Box\ \frac{2}{3}$        b) $\frac{4}{5}\ \Box\ \frac{7}{9}$

   c) $\frac{3}{10}\ \Box\ \frac{2}{7}$        d) $\frac{7}{12}\ \Box\ \frac{3}{5}$

   *4 marks*

5. Work out:

   a) 5453 × 14

   b) 3561 × 35

   2 marks

6. Work out:

   a) 22 ) 9 0 7  r

   b) 31 ) 8 4 7  r

   2 marks

7. Work out:

   a) 823 151 − 7142

   b) 753 172 − 634 714

   2 marks

How did you do?  Score:

# Autumn Term: Workout 12

## Quick Fire

Try to work out the answers to these in your head.

1. a) 6 × 900 = ..............  b) 6200 ÷ 20 = ..............

   c) 14 400 ÷ 12 = ..............  d) 70 × 30 = ..............

   *2 marks*

2. a) $4^2$ = ..............  b) $8^2$ = ..............

   c) $1^3$ = ..............  d) $5^3$ = ..............

   *2 marks*

## Now try these:

3. Work out:

   a) 13 ) 2 8 7 6    r    b) 12 ) 4 9 5 8    r

   *2 marks*

4. Put the fractions below in order from **largest** to **smallest**.

   $\frac{7}{5}$    $\frac{13}{10}$    $\frac{11}{8}$    $\frac{27}{20}$

   largest                                         smallest

   *2 marks*

5. Round:

   a) 6 418 354 to the nearest 1 000 000 ........................

   b) 2 752 941 to the nearest 100 000 ........................

   *2 marks*

6. Work out:

   a) $\frac{7}{48} + \frac{5}{6} = \frac{\square}{\square}$
   
   b) $\frac{4}{5} - \frac{2}{45} = \frac{\square}{\square}$

   *2 marks*

7. Fill in the boxes with **>** or **<** to make the sentences true.

   a) 4 367 106 ☐ 4 367 016

   b) 9 143 722 ☐ 9 145 341

   *2 marks*

8. Work out:

   a) 6108 × 71

   b) 7323 × 23

   *2 marks*

How did you do?   Score: ☐

# Spring Term: Workout 1

**Quick Fire**

Try to work out the answers to these in your head.

1. a) 23 000 × 3 = ..............  b) 1200 × 6 = ..............

   c) 4500 ÷ 9 = ..............  d) 63 000 ÷ 7 = ..............

   *2 marks*

2. a) 18 035 + 560 = ..............  b) 6123 + 3700 = ..............

   c) 34 996 − 604 = ..............  d) 7592 − 4001 = ..............

   *2 marks*

**Now try these:**

3. Work out:

   a) $\frac{1}{3} + \frac{1}{4} = \frac{\Box}{\Box}$   b) $\frac{1}{2} - \frac{1}{9} = \frac{\Box}{\Box}$

   *2 marks*

4. Round:

   a) 5 462 157 to the nearest 10 000 ..............................

   b) 2 589 621 to the nearest 1 000 000 ..............................

   *2 marks*

5. Fill in the missing numbers.

   a) −5 + .......... = 4

   b) .......... − 19 = −22

   c) .......... + 15 = 3

   d) 18 − .......... = −6

   _____
   4 marks

6. Tick the **two** number sentences below that are true.

   7 198 237 > 7 197 329 ☐

   849 225 > 851 663 ☐

   5 896 565 < 6 103 823 ☐

   3 664 298 < 3 656 299 ☐

   _____
   2 marks

7. Give your answers to the calculations below in their simplest form.

   a) $\frac{1}{7} + \frac{2}{3} = \frac{\Box}{\Box}$

   b) $\frac{4}{5} - \frac{1}{3} = \frac{\Box}{\Box}$

   _____
   2 marks

How did you do?

Score: ☐

# Spring Term: Workout 2

## Quick Fire

Try to work out the answers to these in your head.

1.  a) 12 × 5 – 10 = ............    b) 52 – 36 ÷ 6 = ............

    c) (9 + 2) × 8 = ............    d) 81 ÷ (15 – 6) = ............

    *2 marks*

2.  a) 6235 + 203 = ............    b) 2947 + 4999 = ............

    c) 1956 – 398 = ............    d) 4461 – 1005 = ............

    *2 marks*

## Now try these:

3. Work out the following using long division.

    a)      b)

    *2 marks*

4. Fill in the boxes with **>** or **<** to make the sentences true.

    a) 6/5 ☐ 4/3    b) 7/4 ☐ 8/6

    *2 marks*

5. Fill in the missing numbers.

   a) 45 ÷ .............. = 0.045    b) .............. ÷ 100 = 2.03

   c) 6.1 ÷ .............. = 0.061   d) .............. ÷ 1000 = 7.4

   *4 marks*

6. Write the fractions below in their simplest form.

   a) $\dfrac{35}{45} = \dfrac{\Box}{\Box}$    b) $\dfrac{48}{80} = \dfrac{\Box}{\Box}$

   *2 marks*

7. Work out the following using long division.

   a) 31 ⟌ 8 0 6     b) 28 ⟌ 9 2 4

   *2 marks*

How did you do?

Score:

# Spring Term: Workout 3

## Quick Fire

Try to work out the answers to these in your head.

1. a) 41 100 × 2 = ..................  b) 900 × 8 = ..............

   c) 81 000 ÷ 9 = ..............  d) 5400 ÷ 6 = ..............

   *2 marks*

2. a) 0.023 × 100 = ..............  b) 3.55 × 1000 = ..............

   c) 0.48 ÷ 10 = ..............  d) 9.6 ÷ 100 = ..............

   *2 marks*

## Now try these:

3. Work out the calculations below.
   Give your answers as mixed numbers.

   a) $3\frac{1}{2} + \frac{3}{4} = \square\frac{\square}{\square}$    b) $4\frac{1}{3} - \frac{5}{9} = \square\frac{\square}{\square}$

   *2 marks*

4. Work out:

   a) 1.4 × 3 = ..............

   b) 5.2 × 2 = ..............

   *2 marks*

5. Put the fractions below in order from **smallest** to **largest**.

$$\frac{31}{42} \qquad \frac{5}{7} \qquad \frac{2}{3} \qquad \frac{2}{7}$$

smallest                                          largest    2 marks

6. Work out:

   a) 5033 × 31

   b) 1362 × 55

   2 marks

7. Work out:

   a) 0.5 × 13 = ............

   b) 1.7 × 6 = ............

   2 marks

8. Work out the calculations below.
   Give your answers as mixed numbers.

   a) $4\frac{1}{5} - 2\frac{1}{2} =$ ▢ $\frac{▢}{▢}$

   b) $1\frac{1}{6} + 2\frac{2}{5} =$ ▢ $\frac{▢}{▢}$

   2 marks

How did you do?                              Score:

# Spring Term: Workout 4

## Quick Fire

Try to work out the answers to these in your head.

1.  a) 3.41 × 10 = ............    b) 1.689 × 100 = ............

    c) 7.2 × 1000 = ............    d) 0.31 × 1000 = ............

    *2 marks*

2.  a) 7655 − 597 = ............    b) 3084 + 705 = ............

    c) 6492 + 2999 = ............    d) 2135 − 1008 = ............

    *2 marks*

## Now try these:

3. Work out the following using long division.

   a) 16 ) 2 1 6 0

   b) 22 ) 7 0 8 4

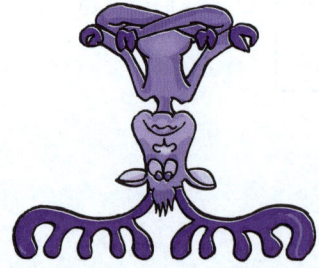

*2 marks*

4. Fill in the missing numbers.

   a) 3 + 5 × .............. = 63

   b) .............. + 2 × 8 = 25

   2 marks

5. Write $\frac{2}{5}$ and $\frac{3}{8}$ as fractions with the same denominator.

   $\frac{2}{5}$ = $\frac{\Box}{\Box}$          $\frac{3}{8}$ = $\frac{\Box}{\Box}$

   2 marks

6. Fill in the missing numbers.

   a) −13 + .......... = 11        b) .......... + 8 = −30

   c) .......... − 24 = −5         d) 20 − .......... = −13

   4 marks

7. Work out the following using long division.

   a)  31 ) 6 6 3 4

   b)  54 ) 7 2 9 0

   2 marks

How did you do?                                   Score:

© CGP — not to be photocopied                                    Spring Term: Workout 4

# Spring Term: Workout 5

## Quick Fire

Try to work out the answers to these in your head.

1. a) 35 + 23 − 12 = ............    b) 100 − 36 + 21 = ............

   c) 68 + 40 − 56 = ............    d) 71 − 38 + 62 = ............

   *2 marks*

2. a) 8000 × 6 = ............    b) 510 × 2 = ............

   c) 60 000 ÷ 5 = ............    d) 7200 ÷ 12 = ............

   *2 marks*

## Now try these:

3. Work out:

   a) $\frac{1}{3} \times \frac{1}{2} = \frac{\square}{\square}$    b) $\frac{1}{4} \times \frac{1}{5} = \frac{\square}{\square}$

   *2 marks*

4. Work out:

   a) 2.07 × 3 = ............    b) 1.32 × 6 = ............

   *2 marks*

5. Put the fractions below in order from **largest** to **smallest**.

$\frac{7}{4}$  $\frac{11}{12}$  $\frac{15}{8}$  $\frac{65}{48}$

largest                    smallest

2 marks

6. Fill in the missing numbers.

a) 5 × ......... ÷ 10 = 3

b) ......... × 8 ÷ 12 = 4

c) ......... ÷ 7 × 9 = 81

d) 121 ÷ 11 × ......... = 110

4 marks

7. Work out:

a) $\frac{2}{5} \times \frac{2}{3} = \frac{\Box}{\Box}$

b) $\frac{5}{6} \times \frac{1}{4} = \frac{\Box}{\Box}$

2 marks

How did you do?

Score:

# Spring Term: Workout 6

## Quick Fire

Try to work out the answers to these in your head.

1. a) 5.53 × 1000 = ............    b) 0.818 × 100 = ............

   c) 4.91 ÷ 10 = ............    d) 7.6 ÷ 100 = ............

   *2 marks*

2. a) 1999 + 486 = ............    b) 7317 − 207 = ............

   c) 4006 + 3998 = ............    d) 5299 − 4020 = ............

   *2 marks*

## Now try these:

3. Work out:

   a) 14 ) 4 5 4    r

   b) 23 ) 5 8 9    r

   *2 marks*

4. Work out the multiplications below.
   Give your answers in their simplest form.

   a) $\frac{1}{4} \times \frac{4}{6} = \frac{\Box}{\Box}$    b) $\frac{2}{5} \times \frac{3}{8} = \frac{\Box}{\Box}$

   *2 marks*

5. Fill in the boxes below to make each fraction equivalent to $\frac{4}{7}$.

a) $\frac{\Box}{28}$

b) $\frac{24}{\Box}$

2 marks

6. Work out:

a) 0.8 × 7 = ..............

b) 5.1 × 4 = ..............

c) 2.9 × 3 = ..............

d) 1.1 × 21 = ..............

4 marks

7. Work out:

a) $\frac{3}{8} + \frac{1}{3} = \frac{\Box}{\Box}$

b) $\frac{5}{6} - \frac{2}{5} = \frac{\Box}{\Box}$

2 marks

How did you do?

Score:

Spring Term: Workout 6

# Spring Term: Workout 7

## Quick Fire

Try to work out the answers to these in your head.

1. a) 120 × 110 = ..................  b) 4000 × 8 = ..................

   c) 84 000 ÷ 7 = ..................  d) 2400 ÷ 60 = ..................

   *2 marks*

2. a) 1.5 × .............. = 1500  b) 0.032 × .............. = 0.32

   c) 5.4 ÷ .............. = 0.054  d) 6.8 ÷ .............. = 0.68

   *4 marks*

## Now try these:

3. Work out:

   a) $\frac{1}{2} \div 3 = \frac{\Box}{\Box}$    b) $\frac{1}{5} \div 4 = \frac{\Box}{\Box}$

   *2 marks*

4. Round:

   a) 2 335 492 to the nearest 1 000 000  ..........................

   b) 629 703 to the nearest 1000  ..........................

   *2 marks*

5. Put the fractions below in order from **smallest** to **largest**.

$$\frac{53}{40} \qquad \frac{17}{10} \qquad \frac{7}{5} \qquad \frac{31}{20}$$

smallest □ □ □ □ largest

2 marks

6. Say whether the number sentences below are **true** or **false**.

18 000 ÷ 900 > 1800 ÷ 9 ..................

200 × 600 < 20 000 × 60 ..................

2 marks

7. Work out:

a) $\frac{3}{5} \div 2 = \frac{\Box}{\Box}$ 	 b) $\frac{3}{7} \div 5 = \frac{\Box}{\Box}$

2 marks

How did you do? 	 Score:

# Spring Term: Workout 8

**Quick Fire**

Try to work out the answers to these in your head.

1. a) 16 + 33 − 8 = ............   b) 48 + 7 − 52 = ............

   c) 94 − 65 + 10 = ............   d) 103 − 5 + 21 = ............

   *2 marks*

2. a) 20 × 300 = ............   b) 8 × 6000 = ............

   c) 120 × 90 = ............   d) 70 × 11 = ............

   *2 marks*

**Now try these:**

3. Use division to write the fractions below as decimals:

   a) $\frac{1}{8}$ = ............   b) $\frac{5}{8}$ = ............

   $8 \overline{)1.000}$   $8 \overline{)5.000}$

   *2 marks*

4. Fill in the boxes with > or < to make the sentences true.

   a) $\frac{11}{7}$ ☐ $\frac{35}{21}$   b) $\frac{42}{32}$ ☐ $\frac{13}{8}$

   *2 marks*

5. Work out:

   a) 3.41 × 4 = ..............   b) 4.08 × 5 = ..............

   2 marks

6. Fill in the missing numbers.

   a) ......... × (4 + 5) = 81   b) ......... ÷ 5 − 6 = 6

   c) ......... + 11 × 3 = 40   d) 36 ÷ (......... − 9) = 3

   4 marks

7. Work out the calculations below.
   Give your answers as mixed numbers.

   a) $2\frac{1}{5} - \frac{3}{4} = \square\frac{\square}{\square}$

   b) $4\frac{2}{7} + 3\frac{1}{3} = \square\frac{\square}{\square}$

   2 marks

How did you do?   Score:

# Spring Term: Workout 9

## Quick Fire

Try to work out the answers to these in your head.

1.  a) ............ ÷ 100 = 8.43      b) ............ ÷ 1000 = 0.27

    c) ............ × 1000 = 66       d) ............ × 10 = 0.81

    *4 marks*

2.  a) 3447 + 899 = ............      b) 4995 − 302 = ............

    c) 7992 + 1210 = ............     d) 1659 − 1007 = ............

    *2 marks*

## Now try these:

3. Work out:

   a) 16.8 ÷ 7      b) 23.4 ÷ 6

   *2 marks*

4. Circle the fractions below that are equivalent to $\frac{3}{5}$.

   $\frac{13}{15}$      $\frac{18}{30}$      $\frac{2}{3}$      $\frac{9}{16}$      $\frac{27}{45}$      $\frac{34}{60}$

   *2 marks*

5. Work out:

   a) 223 × 84

   b) 4309 × 59

   2 marks

6. Fill in the missing fractions in the calculations below.

   a) $\frac{1}{5} \times \frac{\square}{\square} = \frac{3}{20}$

   b) $\frac{3}{8} \times \frac{\square}{\square} = \frac{9}{56}$

   2 marks

7. Work out:

   a) 44.7 ÷ 3

   b) 89.6 ÷ 7

   2 marks

How did you do?

Score:

# Spring Term: Workout 10

## Quick Fire

Try to work out the answers to these in your head.

1. a) 35 − 22 + 46 = ............   b) 137 − 55 + 13 = ............

   c) 41 + 47 − 39 = ............   d) 83 + 72 − 33 = ............

   *2 marks*

2. a) ............ + 3001 = 5002   b) 8002 − ............ = 6003

   c) 3044 + ............ = 7043   d) ............ − 4003 = 1006

   *4 marks*

## Now try these:

3. Work out:

   a) 12 ⟌ 1 6 2 6   r      b) 25 ⟌ 5 7 8 0   r

   *2 marks*

4. Work out:

   a) 7.85 ÷ 5      b) 29.12 ÷ 8

   5 ⟌ 7.8 5

   *2 marks*

5. Work out:

a) $\frac{2}{3} \div 5 = \frac{\square}{\square}$

b) $\frac{3}{4} \div 7 = \frac{\square}{\square}$

2 marks

6. Put the fractions below in order from **largest** to **smallest**.

$\frac{5}{3}$   $\frac{11}{6}$   $\frac{13}{8}$   $\frac{21}{12}$

largest □ □ □ □ smallest

2 marks

7. Work out the multiplications below.
Give your answers in their simplest form.

a) $\frac{4}{5} \times \frac{5}{8} = \frac{\square}{\square}$

b) $\frac{2}{7} \times \frac{7}{12} = \frac{\square}{\square}$

2 marks

How did you do?

Score:

# Spring Term: Workout 11

## Quick Fire

Try to work out the answers to these in your head.

1. a) 46 ÷ (19 + 4) = ............   b) 8 × 8 + 4 = ............

   c) 23 − 15 ÷ 3 = ............   d) 70 ÷ (12 − 5) = ............

   *2 marks*

2. a) 3600 ÷ 12 = ............   b) 60 × 70 = ............

   c) 12 100 ÷ 11 = ............   d) 200 × 80 = ............

   *2 marks*

## Now try these:

3. Write the fractions below as percentages:

   a) $\frac{7}{20}$ = ............ %   b) $\frac{33}{50}$ = ............ %

   c) $\frac{23}{25}$ = ............ %   d) $\frac{12}{25}$ = ............ %

   *4 marks*

4. Round:

   a) 5 765 008 to the nearest 10 000   ............

   b) 809 722 to the nearest 1000   ............

   *2 marks*

5. Work out:

   a) 1.32 × 7 = ..............
   
   b) 13 × 3.1 = ..............
   
   2 marks

6. Tick the number sentences below that are true.

   45% = $\frac{9}{20}$ ☐
   
   0.32 = 3.2% ☐
   
   $\frac{4}{25}$ = 0.25 ☐
   
   98% = 0.98 ☐
   
   2 marks

7. Work out:

   a) 35 ) 7 8 4 5   r
   
   b) 23 ) 4 6 3 2   r
   
   2 marks

How did you do?

Score: ☐

# Spring Term: Workout 12

**Quick Fire**

Try to work out the answers to these in your head.

1. a) 12 084 + 502 = .............   b) 5761 − 499 = .............

   c) 24 339 − 3004 = .............   d) 3914 + 1997 = .............

   *2 marks*

2. a) 10 × 6 ÷ 5 = .............   b) 32 ÷ 4 × 9 = .............

   c) 49 ÷ 7 × 0 = .............   d) 6 × 9 ÷ 3 = .............

   *2 marks*

**Now try these:**

3. Work out:

   a) 10% of 50 .............   b) 30% of 30 .............

   c) 50% of 72 .............   d) 80% of 60 .............

   *4 marks*

4. Work out the calculations below. Give your answers as mixed numbers in their simplest form.

   a) $1\frac{3}{8} + 2\frac{5}{6} =$ ☐$\frac{☐}{☐}$   b) $3\frac{1}{6} - \frac{7}{9} =$ ☐$\frac{☐}{☐}$

   *2 marks*

5. Work out:

   a) 23.2 ÷ 4 = ..............    b) 43.56 ÷ 9 = ..............

   4 | 2 3.2            9 | 4 3.5 6

   2 marks

6. Work out:

   a) 15% of 80    b) 65% of 120

   10% = ..............

   5% = ..............

   15% = ..............              65% = ..............

   2 marks

7. Use division to write the fractions below as decimals:

   a) $\frac{3}{8}$ = ..............    b) $\frac{7}{8}$ = ..............

   8 | 3.0 0 0          8 | 7.0 0 0

   2 marks

How did you do?  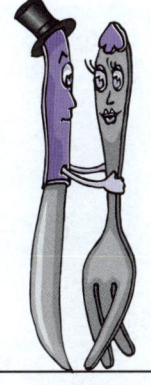  Score:

# Summer Term: Workout 1

## Quick Fire

Try to work out the answers to these in your head.

1. a) 53 165 ÷ 1000 = ..........................................

   b) 85 300 ÷ 1000 = ..........................................

   c) 246 570 ÷ 1000 = ..........................................

   d) 54 046 ÷ 1000 = ..........................................

   *2 marks*

2. Work out:

   a) $\dfrac{1}{3} \times \dfrac{1}{4} = \dfrac{\Box}{\Box}$
   
   b) $\dfrac{1}{6} \times \dfrac{5}{7} = \dfrac{\Box}{\Box}$

   *2 marks*

## Now try these:

3. Work out:

   a) 23 − 40 = ............
   
   b) 15 − 33 = ............

   c) −42 + 57 = ............
   
   d) −23 + 39 = ............

   *4 marks*

4. Put the numbers below in order from smallest to largest.

   1 546 464     1 556 464     1 546 564     1 546 465

   ............... ............... ............... ...............
   smallest                                    largest

   *2 marks*

5. Work out:

   a) 0.5 × 4 = ............    b) 0.8 × 3 = ............

   c) 0.2 × 9 = ............    d) 0.4 × 7 = ............

   *2 marks*

6. Work out:

   a) $\dfrac{15}{16} - \dfrac{3}{4} = \dfrac{\Box}{\Box}$     b) $\dfrac{17}{24} - \dfrac{1}{6} = \dfrac{\Box}{\Box}$

   *2 marks*

7. Use long division to work out:

   a) 3584 ÷ 14     b) 5625 ÷ 25

   14 ⟌ 3 5 8 4        25 ⟌ 5 6 2 5

   *2 marks*

How did you do?          Score:

# Summer Term: Workout 2

## Quick Fire

Try to work out the answers to these in your head.

1. a) 2536 + 4080 = ............    b) 1457 + 4008 = ............

   c) 3145 + 3500 = ............    d) 5236 + 2090 = ............

   *2 marks*

2. Count **forwards** in steps of 4 to fill in the missing numbers.

   −11    −7    ............    ............    ............

   *1 mark*

## Now try these:

3. Work out:

   a) $\frac{1}{5} \div 2 = \frac{\Box}{\Box}$    b) $\frac{1}{3} \div 6 = \frac{\Box}{\Box}$

   *2 marks*

4. Fill in the missing values in these equivalent fractions.

   $\frac{4}{5} = \frac{\Box}{20} = \frac{36}{\Box}$

   *1 mark*

5. Work out the following divisions using long division.

   a)  11 ⟌ 6 2 3     r

   b)  12 ⟌ 9 0 6     r

   2 marks

6. Work out:

   a) 8 ÷ 2 − 4 = ..............

   b) 5 + 2 × 3 = ..............

   c) 14 + 8 ÷ 4 = ..............

   3 marks

7. Work out:

   a) $\frac{1}{7} + \frac{3}{4} = \frac{\Box}{\Box}$

   b) $\frac{2}{5} + \frac{1}{6} = \frac{\Box}{\Box}$

   2 marks

8. What is:

   a) 25% of 84? ................

   b) 70% of 600? ................

   c) 95% of 460? ................

   3 marks

How did you do?

Score:

# Summer Term: Workout 3

## Quick Fire

Try to work out the answers to these in your head.

1. Write the fractions below in their simplest form.

   a) $\frac{18}{90} \rightarrow \frac{\Box}{\Box}$
   
   b) $\frac{24}{72} \rightarrow \frac{\Box}{\Box}$

   *2 marks*

2. a) 0.06 × 11 = ..............
   
   b) 0.09 × 8 = ..............

   *2 marks*

## Now try these:

3. a) 8878 − 7600 = ..............

   b) 6503 − 2090 = ..............

   c) 8325 − 6006 = ..............

   *3 marks*

4. Count **backwards** in steps of 6 to fill in the missing numbers.

   11    5    ..........    ..........    ..........    ..........

   *2 marks*

5. Work out:

   a) 419 × 16

   b) 253 × 32

   *2 marks*

6. Write in the missing numbers in the equivalent fractions, decimals and percentages:

   a) $\frac{3}{20}$ = 0.............. = ..............%

   b) $\frac{\square}{8}$ = 0.375 = ..............%

   c) $\frac{\square}{50}$ = 0.............. = 82%

   *3 marks*

7. Work out these divisions using short division. Give your answers as decimals.

   a) 9 ÷ 4

   b) 12 ÷ 5

   *2 marks*

How did you do?  Score:

# Summer Term: Workout 4

## Quick Fire

Try to work out the answers to these in your head.

1. Put the numbers below in order from largest to smallest.

   446 123      464 123      466 123      446 234

   .................   .................   .................   .................
   largest                                        smallest

   *1 mark*

2. a) ............ × 7 = 0.42      b) 0.06 × ............ = 0.36

   c) 0.09 × ............ = 0.45   d) ............ × 5 = 0.4

   *4 marks*

## Now try these:

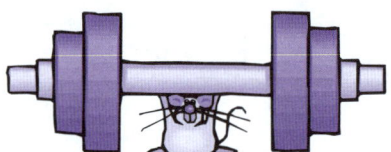

3. Give your answers to the following multiplications as improper fractions in their simplest form:

   a) $\frac{5}{6} \times 8 = \frac{\Box}{\Box}$   b) $\frac{5}{8} \times 2 = \frac{\Box}{\Box}$   c) $\frac{7}{12} \times 3 = \frac{\Box}{\Box}$

   *3 marks*

4. Work out:

   a)  2457 × 34

   b)  8704 × 26

   _____
   2 marks

5. Circle the largest fraction and draw a box around the smallest.

   $\frac{31}{36}$ $\qquad$ $\frac{8}{9}$ $\qquad$ $\frac{5}{6}$ $\qquad$ $\frac{17}{18}$

   _____
   2 marks

6. Give your answers to the following additions as improper fractions in their simplest form:

   a)  $3\frac{1}{2} + \frac{3}{4} = \frac{\Box}{\Box}$
   
   b)  $4\frac{1}{6} + \frac{5}{3} = \frac{\Box}{\Box}$

   _____
   2 marks

7. Fill in the boxes with > or < to make the sentences true.

   a)  $\frac{23}{25}$ $\Box$ 0.91
   
   b)  $\frac{17}{20}$ $\Box$ 86%

   _____
   2 marks

How did you do?                       Score: [ ]

# Summer Term: Workout 5

## Quick Fire

Try to work out the answers to these in your head.

1. Fill in the boxes with **>** or **<** to make the sentences true.

   a) $1\frac{5}{6}$ ☐ $\frac{13}{6}$   b) $1\frac{2}{3}$ ☐ $\frac{4}{3}$

   *1 mark*

2. a) −18 + 23 = ……….   b) 7 − 20 = ……….

   c) −13 + 30 = ……….   d) −4 − 28 = ……….

   *4 marks*

## Now try these:

3. Write the improper fractions below in their simplest form.

   a) $\frac{21}{18} \rightarrow \frac{\square}{\square}$   b) $\frac{42}{28} \rightarrow \frac{\square}{\square}$

   *2 marks*

4. Count **forwards** in steps of $\frac{3}{100}$ to fill in the missing numbers, giving your answers in their simplest form.

   $\frac{51}{100}$   $\frac{27}{50}$   $\frac{\square}{100}$   $\frac{\square}{5}$   $\frac{63}{100}$

   *2 marks*

5. Work out:

   a) 6 + 5 × 8 + 2 = ............

   b) (6 + 5) × 8 + 2 = ............

   c) (6 + 5) × (8 + 2) = ............

3 marks

6. Work out the following divisions using long division. Use remainders where appropriate.

   a) 702 ÷ 13
   
   b) 1656 ÷ 24

2 marks

7. Give your answers to the following additions as improper fractions in their simplest form:

   a) $\frac{6}{7} + \frac{4}{21} = \frac{\Box}{\Box}$
   
   b) $\frac{4}{5} + \frac{1}{2} = \frac{\Box}{\Box}$

2 marks

How did you do?

Score:

# Summer Term: Workout 6

## Quick Fire

Try to work out the answers to these in your head.

1. a) 0.03 × 20 = ..............  b) 0.05 × 50 = ..............

   c) 0.9 × 400 = ..............  d) 600 × 0.07 = ..............

   *2 marks*

2. a) 0.07 ÷ 10 = ..............  b) 1.09 ÷ 10 = ..............

   c) 38 ÷ 100 = ..............  d) 16.2 ÷ 100 = ..............

   e) 269 ÷ 1000 = ..............  f) 1503 ÷ 1000 = ..............

   *3 marks*

## Now try these:

3. Write in the missing numbers in the equivalent fractions, decimals and percentages:

   a) .............. = $\frac{5}{8}$ = ..............%

   b) ..............% = 0.52 = $\frac{\square}{25}$

   *2 marks*

4. Work out:

   a) 2440 ÷ 2 = ..............   b) 1209 ÷ 3 = ..............

   c) 1020 ÷ 5 = ..............   d) 6054 ÷ 6 = ..............

   *4 marks*

5. Work out:

   a) 26 − 34 = ..............

   b) 18 − 27 = ..............

   *1 mark*

6. Work out the divisions below, giving your answers as decimals.

   a) 203 ÷ 5   b) 619 ÷ 5

   *2 marks*

7. Give your answers to the following multiplications in their simplest form:

   a) $\frac{5}{8} \times \frac{2}{5} = \frac{\square}{\square}$   b) $\frac{4}{7} \times \frac{3}{8} = \frac{\square}{\square}$

   *2 marks*

**How did you do?**          **Score:**

# Summer Term: Workout 7

## Quick Fire

Try to work out the answers to these in your head.

1.  a) 6151 + 2600 = ..............   b) 2849 + 6800 = ..............

    c) 8437 − 1900 = ..............   d) 5352 − 4400 = ..............

    *2 marks*

2.  a) 1.35 × 100 = ..............    b) 1.006 × 100 = ..............

    c) 0.512 × 1000 = ..............  d) 9.02 × 1000 = ..............

    *2 marks*

## Now try these:

3. Write the fractions below in their simplest form.

    a) $\frac{25}{35} = \frac{\Box}{\Box}$    b) $\frac{18}{48} = \frac{\Box}{\Box}$    c) $\frac{27}{45} = \frac{\Box}{\Box}$

    *3 marks*

4. Circle the fraction below that is equivalent to 45%.

    $\frac{45}{50}$    $\frac{19}{20}$    $\frac{18}{40}$    $\frac{5}{8}$

    *1 mark*

5. What is:

   a) 20% of 50?  .................

   b) 55% of 80?  .................

   c) 90% of 130?  .................

   d) 35% of 240?  .................

   4 marks

6. Put the fractions below in order from **largest** to **smallest**.

   $\frac{4}{7}$     $\frac{19}{28}$     $\frac{3}{4}$     $\frac{9}{14}$

   largest                                    smallest

   2 marks

7. Work out the following divisions using long division.
   Use remainders where appropriate.

   a) 4940 ÷ 24          b) 5510 ÷ 15

   2 marks

How did you do?                    Score:

# Summer Term: Workout 8

## Quick Fire

Try to work out the answers to these in your head.

1. a) 3600 ÷ 40 = ................   b) 10 800 ÷ 12 = ................

   c) 7 × 1100 = ................   d) 30 × 600 = ................

   *2 marks*

2. a) 4 − 7 = ................   b) 9 − 13 = ................

   c) −6 − 2 = ................   d) −7 − 9 = ................

   *4 marks*

## Now try these:

3. Round:

   a) 6 058 454 to the nearest 100 000.   ........................

   b) 91 554 to the nearest 100.   ........................

   *2 marks*

4. Write the fractions below as percentages:

   a) $\frac{7}{20}$ = ................ %   b) $\frac{24}{25}$ = ................ %

   *2 marks*

5. Work out:

   a) $\dfrac{7}{12} + \dfrac{2}{5} = \dfrac{\Box}{\Box}$
   
   b) $\dfrac{8}{9} + \dfrac{5}{6} = \dfrac{\Box}{\Box}$

   *2 marks*

6. Work out:

   a) 931 × 22
   
   b) 1362 × 55

   *2 marks*

7. Give your answers to the following multiplications in their simplest form:

   a) $\dfrac{3}{8} \times 6 = \dfrac{\Box}{\Box}$
   
   b) $\dfrac{2}{9} \times 15 = \dfrac{\Box}{\Box}$

   *2 marks*

How did you do?    Score:

# Summer Term: Workout 9

## Quick Fire

Try to work out the answers to these in your head.

1. a) 3264 + 550 = ...............   b) 3691 + 704 = ...............

   c) 7840 + 620 = ...............   d) 7736 + 401 = ...............

   *2 marks*

2. Write the fractions below as decimals:

   a) $\frac{1}{8}$ = ...............   b) $\frac{7}{8}$ = ...............

   *2 marks*

## Now try these:

3. Fill in the missing number:

   a) –8 + ........... = 3   b) ........... – 16 = –27

   c) ........... + 17 = 2   d) 9 – ........... = –11

   *4 marks*

4. Work out:

   a) 8 + 6 ÷ 3 – 7 = ...............

   b) 2 × (5 + 7) ÷ 4 = ...............

   *2 marks*

5. Give your answers to the following additions in their simplest form:

   a) $\frac{1}{11} + \frac{3}{5} = \frac{\Box}{\Box}$

   b) $\frac{7}{12} + \frac{2}{9} = \frac{\Box}{\Box}$

   *2 marks*

6. Work out:

   a) $51 \div 4$

   b) $47 \div 20$

   $4 \overline{\smash{)}5\ 1\ .\ 0\ 0}$

   *2 marks*

7. Give your answers to the following multiplications in their simplest form:

   a) $\frac{7}{9} \times \frac{3}{5} = \frac{\Box}{\Box}$

   b) $\frac{5}{12} \times \frac{4}{7} = \frac{\Box}{\Box}$

   *2 marks*

How did you do?

Score:

# Summer Term: Workout 10

## Quick Fire

Try to work out the answers to these in your head.

1.  a) 9.3 ÷ 100 = ............   b) 36.1 ÷ 100 = ............

    c) 18 200 ÷ 1000 = ............   d) 2014 ÷ 1000 = ............

    *2 marks*

2.  a) 5134 + ............ = 7234   b) 3615 + ............ = 8115

    c) ............ + 1800 = 3261   d) ............ + 5400 = 9538

    *4 marks*

## Now try these:

3.  Circle the largest fraction and draw a box around the smallest.

    $\frac{2}{3}$        $\frac{5}{8}$        $\frac{5}{6}$        $\frac{3}{4}$

    *2 marks*

4.  Write the fractions below in their simplest form.

    a) $\frac{180}{288}$ = ☐   b) $\frac{84}{126}$ = ☐

    *2 marks*

5. Work out:

   a) 68.8 ÷ 4 = ..............   b) 46.2 ÷ 7 = ..............

   *2 marks*

6. Give your answers to the following multiplications in their simplest form:

   a) $\frac{6}{7} \times \frac{2}{3} = \frac{\Box}{\Box}$   b) $\frac{15}{22} \times \frac{4}{5} = \frac{\Box}{\Box}$

   *2 marks*

7. Work out the following divisions using long division.

   a) 8595 ÷ 21   b) 7720 ÷ 31

   21 ⟌ 8 5 9 5    r

   *2 marks*

**How did you do?**

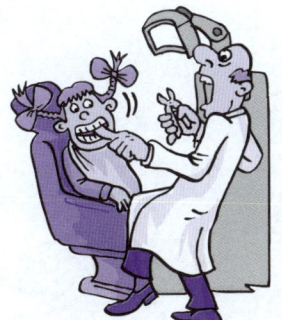

**Score:**

# Summer Term: Workout 11

## Quick Fire

Try to work out the answers to these in your head.

1. a) 101 × 5 = ............    b) 201 × 11 = ............

   c) 6408 ÷ 8 = ............    d) 1224 ÷ 12 = ............

   *4 marks*

2. Work out:

   a) $\frac{2}{5} + \frac{3}{10} = \frac{\Box}{\Box}$    b) $\frac{18}{20} - \frac{3}{4} = \frac{\Box}{\Box}$

   *2 marks*

## Now try these:

3. Fill in the boxes with > or < to make the sentences true.

   a) $\frac{10}{9}$ □ $\frac{41}{36}$    b) $\frac{55}{49}$ □ $\frac{8}{7}$

   *2 marks*

4. Work out:

   $(14 - 5) \times 2^2$ = ............

   *1 mark*

5. What is:

   a) 15% of 600? ..............

   b) 35% of 3200? ..............

   c) 85% of 1500? ..............

   3 marks

6. Write in the missing numbers in the equivalent fractions, decimals and percentages:

   a) $\frac{12}{25}$ = 0. .............. = .............. %

   b) $\frac{\square}{8}$ = 0. .............. = 87.5%

   2 marks

7. Work out:

   a) 223 × 84          b) 4309 × 59

   2 marks

How did you do?     Score:

# Summer Term: Workout 12

## Quick Fire

Try to work out the answers to these in your head.

1. a) 0.07 × 50 = ............   b) 0.09 × 30 = ............

   c) 0.03 × 80 = ............   d) 0.05 × 11 = ............

   *2 marks*

2. a) 10% of 30? ............   b) 50% of 16? ............

   c) 1% of 200? ............   d) 25% of 80? ............

   *4 marks*

## Now try these:

3. Work out:

   a) $\frac{7}{11} + \frac{1}{4} = \frac{\Box}{\Box}$   b) $\frac{8}{9} - \frac{6}{7} = \frac{\Box}{\Box}$

   *2 marks*

4. Work out:

   a) 7.01 × 8 = ............   b) 0.49 × 5 = ............

   *2 marks*

5.  Work out:

    a)  3 + (9 − 5) × 12 = ..............

    b)  10 − 3 + 8 ÷ 2 = ..............

2 marks

6.  Work out the following divisions using long division. Use remainders where appropriate.

    a)  702 ÷ 13

    b)  9954 ÷ 16

2 marks

7.  Give your answers to the following divisions in their simplest form:

    a)  $\frac{6}{7} \div 12 = \frac{\Box}{\Box}$

    b)  $\frac{15}{17} \div 5 = \frac{\Box}{\Box}$

2 marks

How did you do?   Score:

# Puzzle: Fractional Footpaths

You've finished the workouts! Practise your skills by solving this puzzle.

The map below shows the lengths, in miles, of the paths between James' house and the beach.
He can only walk along the paths in the direction of the arrows.

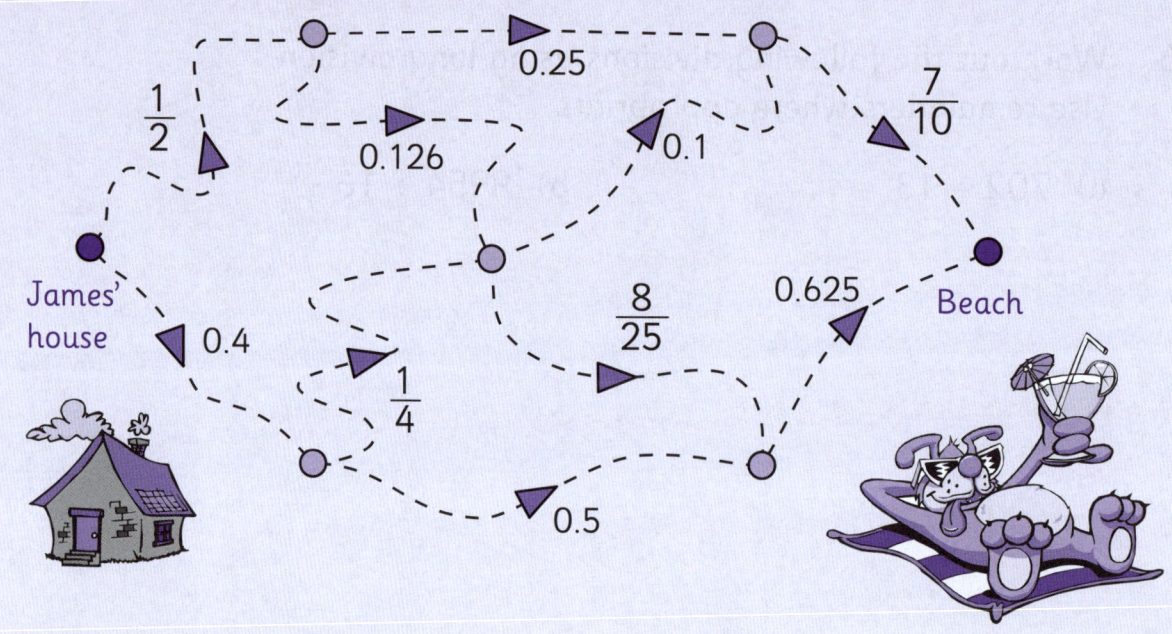

Can you find the shortest and longest routes from James' house to the beach?

Shortest = .............. miles

Longest = .............. miles

**Puzzle Complete?**

Puzzle: Fractional Footpaths

# Answers

## Autumn Term

### Workout 1 — pages 2-3

1. a) **10 812**  b) **8546**
   c) **6063**  d) **4221**
   2 marks for all four correct,
   otherwise 1 mark for at least two correct

2. a) **5.4**  b) **123**  c) **49**  d) **0.71**
   2 marks for all four correct,
   otherwise 1 mark for at least two correct

3. a) **460 000**  b) **500 000**
   1 mark for each correct answer

4. a) $\frac{9}{10}$  1 mark   b) $\frac{53}{100}$  1 mark

5. 183 657   **173 657**   **163 657**   153 657
   2 marks for all three correct,
   otherwise 1 mark for two correct

6. a) **25**  1 mark
   b) **49**  1 mark

7. a) 775 445 **>** 775 384  1 mark
   b) 348 761 **<** 384 671  1 mark

8. a)  156 023       b)  367 119
     + 435 782          +  41 543
     ─────────           ─────────
       **591 805**         **408 662**
          1 1                   1 1
   1 mark for each correct answer

### Workout 2 — pages 4-5

1. a) **36 842**   b) **36 891**
   c) **27 063**   d) **11 054**
   2 marks for all four correct,
   otherwise 1 mark for at least two correct

2. a) **0.38**  b) **0.95**  c) **155**  d) **37**
   2 marks for all four correct,
   otherwise 1 mark for at least two correct

3. a) $\frac{4}{8} = \frac{8}{16}$, so $\frac{4}{8} < \frac{9}{16}$   1 mark
   b) $\frac{5}{7} = \frac{25}{35}$, so $\frac{24}{35} < \frac{5}{7}$   1 mark

4. a) **8**  1 mark    b) **64**  1 mark

5. a) **$2\frac{4}{5}$**  1 mark    b) **$3\frac{3}{8}$**  1 mark

6. a)   ²3̸⁸⁴⁵6̸¹17     b)   ⁶7̸¹²7̸.¹83
      − 193.546           −  35.243
      ─────────           ─────────
        **191.071**         **691.940**
   1 mark for each correct answer

7. a) **0.8**  1 mark   b) **0.56**  1 mark

8. a)    264        b)    367
       ×  35             ×  42
       ─────             ─────
       1 3₃2₂0            7₁3₁4
       7₁9₁2 0           1 4₂6₂8 0
       ─────             ─────
       **9240**           **15414**
         1                 1 1
   1 mark for each correct answer

### Workout 3 — pages 6-7

1. a) **145**  b) **700**  c) **21**  d) **20**
   2 marks for all four correct,
   otherwise 1 mark for at least two correct

2. a) **840**  b) **4500**  c) **7.7**  d) **0.16**
   2 marks for all four correct,
   otherwise 1 mark for at least two correct

3. 34   14   **−6**   **−26**   **−46**
   2 marks for all three correct,
   otherwise 1 mark for two correct

4. a) $\frac{67}{100}$  1 mark    b) **0.67**  1 mark

5. a) **5**  1 mark    b) **8.7**  1 mark

6. a) $\frac{2}{3} + \frac{11}{12} = \frac{8}{12} + \frac{11}{12} = \frac{19}{12} = \mathbf{1\frac{7}{12}}$
   b) $\frac{3}{4} + \frac{7}{8} = \frac{6}{8} + \frac{7}{8} = \frac{13}{8} = \mathbf{1\frac{5}{8}}$
   1 mark for each correct answer

7. **4.341**   **4.35**   **4.358**   **4.4**
   2 marks for all four correct, otherwise
   1 mark for three in the correct order

8. a)      **76**         b)       **137**
       7)5⁵3⁴2                  8)1¹0²9⁵6
   1 mark for each correct answer

### Workout 4 — pages 8-9

1. a) **3524**  b) **7315**  c) **2658**  d) **9026**
   2 marks for all four correct,
   otherwise 1 mark for at least two correct

2. a) **408**   b) **300**   c) **106**   d) **50**
   2 marks for all four correct,
   otherwise 1 mark for at least two correct

3. **3 716 441, 3 687 045, 3 684 228, 3 684 219**
   2 marks for all four correct, otherwise
   1 mark for three in the correct order

4. a) **560.1**  1 mark   b) **0.192**  1 mark
   c) **284**  1 mark   d) **0.035**  1 mark

5. a)    2 7 9 . 3 6 0       b)    3 7 8 . 0 5 9
       + 5 7 . 2 6 8           + 5 8 2 . 9 3 0
         **3 3 6 . 6 2 8**         **9 6 0 . 9 8 9**
            1 1 1                    1 1
   1 mark for each correct answer

6. a) **$2\frac{1}{10}$**  1 mark   b) **$11\frac{1}{5}$**  1 mark

7. a)      **1 3 7**       b)      **6 7 2**
       6 ⟌ 8²2²2            7 ⟌ 4 4⁷5⁰1⁴
   1 mark for each correct answer

## Workout 5 — pages 10-11

1. a) **4.2**   b) **2.3**   c) **0.75**   d) **810**
   2 marks for all four correct,
   otherwise 1 mark for at least two correct

2. a) **693**   b) **255**   c) **101**   d) **2001**
   2 marks for all four correct,
   otherwise 1 mark for at least two correct

3. a) **6 000 000**  1 mark
   b) **3 520 000**  1 mark

4. a) **−3**  1 mark   b) **2**  1 mark
   c) **5**  1 mark    d) **6**  1 mark

5. **6 727 154, 7 327 910, 7 346 637, 7 346 804**
   2 marks for all four correct, otherwise
   1 mark for three in the correct order

6. a) **0.4**  1 mark   b) **0.55**  1 mark

7. a)     5 7 1 6        b)     2 7 3 9
       ×       6              ×       3
         **3 4 2 9 6**           **8 2 1 7**
            4 3                    2 1 2
   1 mark for each correct answer

## Workout 6 — pages 12-13

1. a) **406**   b) **203**   c) **6300**   d) **1860**
   2 marks for all four correct,
   otherwise 1 mark for at least two correct

2. a) **17.2**   b) **0.024**   c) **0.186**   d) **511.7**
   2 marks for all four correct,
   otherwise 1 mark for at least two correct

3. a)    **3 6**            b)    **4 3**
       11 ⟌ 3 ³9 ⁶6         15 ⟌ 6 ⁶4 ⁵5
   1 mark for each correct answer

4. a) **17**  1 mark   b) **22**  1 mark
   c) **16**  1 mark   d) **54**  1 mark

5. a)    4 2 5 . 5 4 0       b)   ⁷8 ¹2 3 . 2 8 8
       + 3 9 0 . 4 5 1          − 1 7 0 . 2 3 0
         **8 1 5 . 9 9 1**         **6 5 3 . 0 5 8**
              1
   1 mark for each correct answer

6. a) **$1\frac{1}{25}$**  1 mark   b) **$1\frac{7}{18}$**  1 mark

7. a)       **2 9 8**        b)        **3 3 1**
       12 ⟌ 3 ³5 ¹¹7 ⁹6        9 ⟌ 2 ²9 ²7 9
   1 mark for each correct answer

## Workout 7 — pages 14-15

1. a) **607.8**   b) **810**
   c) **3.007**   d) **0.061**
   2 marks for all four correct,
   otherwise 1 mark for at least two correct

2. a) **220**   b) **1212**   c) **106**   d) **102**
   2 marks for all four correct,
   otherwise 1 mark for at least two correct

3. a) 24 ÷ (9 − 3) = 24 ÷ 6 = **4**  1 mark
   b) 16 + 5 × 12 = 16 + 60 = **76**  1 mark

4. a) 2 957 349 < 2 961 327  1 mark
   b) 8 818 613 > 8 781 944  1 mark

5. a) **$\frac{51}{100}$**  1 mark   b) **0.51**  1 mark

6. a) **5 310 000**  1 mark
   b) **5 000 000**  1 mark

7. a) **$\frac{11}{36}$**  1 mark   b) **$\frac{9}{32}$**  1 mark

8. a) (7 + 33) ÷ 4 = 40 ÷ 4 = **10**  1 mark
   b) 20 − 10 × 3 = 20 − 30 = **−10**  1 mark

## Workout 8 — pages 16-17

1. a) **72 078**   b) **72 482**
   c) **45 337**   d) **3194**
   2 marks for all four correct,
   otherwise 1 mark for at least two correct

2. a) **0.049**   b) **0.075**   c) **62**   d) **544.1**
   2 marks for all four correct,
   otherwise 1 mark for at least two correct

Answers

3.  a) $\phantom{12\overline{)}}203$
    $12\overline{)2\,{}^24\,{}^36}$
    b) $\phantom{11\overline{)}}603$
    $11\overline{)6\,{}^63\,{}^33}$
    
    1 mark for each correct answer

4.  a) **3000** 1 mark    b) **4800** 1 mark
    c) **600** 1 mark    d) **30** 1 mark

5.  a) **−4** 1 mark    b) **3** 1 mark

6.  a) $\phantom{0}647$
    $\times\phantom{00}37$
    $\overline{\phantom{0}45\,{}_32\,{}_49}$
    $19{,}4{,}210$
    $\overline{23939}$
    $\phantom{00000}1$
    
    b) $\phantom{0}865$
    $\times\phantom{00}31$
    $\overline{\phantom{0}865}$
    $25{,}950$
    $\overline{26815}$
    $\phantom{0000}1\,1$
    
    1 mark for each correct answer

7.  a) $\phantom{12\overline{)}}411$
    $12\overline{)4\,{}^49\,{}^13\,{}^12}$
    b) $\phantom{13\overline{)}}213$
    $13\overline{)2\,{}^27\,{}^16\,{}^39}$
    
    1 mark for each correct answer

## Workout 9 — pages 18-19

1.  a) **17**  b) **30**  c) **28**  d) **66**
    2 marks for all four correct,
    otherwise 1 mark for at least two correct

2.  a) **2101**  b) **0.93**  c) **0.037**  d) **0.188**
    2 marks for all four correct,
    otherwise 1 mark for at least two correct

3.  a) $\phantom{0}2092$
    $\times\phantom{000}24$
    $\overline{\phantom{0}8368}$
    $41{,}840$
    $\overline{50208}$
    $\phantom{000}1\,1\,1$
    
    b) $\phantom{0}1263$
    $\times\phantom{000}71$
    $\overline{\phantom{0}1263}$
    $8{,}84{,}210$
    $\overline{89673}$
    
    1 mark for each correct answer

4.  a) **78%** 1 mark    b) **35%** 1 mark

5.  a) **7** 1 mark    b) **4.3** 1 mark

6.  a) $\dfrac{19}{21}$ 1 mark    b) $\dfrac{7}{36}$ 1 mark

7.  a) $3\dfrac{1}{8}$ 1 mark    b) $10\dfrac{1}{5}$ 1 mark

8.  a) $\phantom{15\overline{)}}17$
    $15\overline{)2\,{}^25\,{}^{10}5}$
    b) $\phantom{18\overline{)}}148$
    $18\overline{)2\,{}^26\,{}^86\,{}^{14}4}$
    
    1 mark for each correct answer

## Workout 10 — pages 20-21

1.  a) **−5**  b) **5**  c) **−17**  d) **18**
    2 marks for all four correct,
    otherwise 1 mark for at least two correct

2.  a) $\dfrac{2}{3}$ 1 mark    b) $\dfrac{3}{4}$ 1 mark

3.  $\dfrac{21}{28} = \dfrac{3}{4}$ and $\dfrac{20}{32} = \dfrac{5}{8}$ should be ticked.
    1 mark for each correct answer.
    Lose a mark for an incorrect answer

4.  a) $\phantom{12\overline{)}}43\,r\,5$
    $12\overline{)5\,{}^52\,{}^41}$
    b) $\phantom{11\overline{)}}63\,r\,4$
    $11\overline{)6\,{}^69\,{}^37}$
    
    1 mark for each correct answer

5.  a) $\phantom{0}975654$
    $+\phantom{0}53351$
    $\overline{1029005}$
    $\phantom{000}1\phantom{00}1\,1$
    
    b) $\phantom{0}641.696$
    $+\phantom{00}65.385$
    $\overline{\phantom{0}707.081}$
    $\phantom{000}1\phantom{0}1\,1\,1$
    
    1 mark for each correct answer

6.  a) $4 \times (8 - 3) = 4 \times 5 =$ **20**  1 mark
    b) $2 + 8 \div 4 = 2 + 2 =$ **4**  1 mark
    c) $28 \div (7 \times 2) = 28 \div 14 =$ **2**  1 mark
    d) $35 - 25 \div 5 = 35 - 5 =$ **30**  1 mark

7.  a) $\phantom{0}{}^4\!5\,{}^{12}\!3\,{}^12\,{}^12\,16$
    $-\phantom{0}38026$
    $\overline{\phantom{0}494190}$
    
    b) $\phantom{0}4\,{}^6\!7\,{}^{18}\!9.8\,{}^14\,0$
    $-\phantom{0}209.925$
    $\overline{\phantom{0}269.915}$
    
    1 mark for each correct answer

## Workout 11 — pages 22-23

1.  a) **24 000**  b) **40**
    c) **600**  d) **9600**
    2 marks for all four correct,
    otherwise 1 mark for at least two correct

2.  a) **3850**  b) **0.072**
    c) **899.4**  d) **0.626**
    2 marks for all four correct,
    otherwise 1 mark for at least two correct

3.  a) $\dfrac{15}{18}$ 1 mark    b) $\dfrac{30}{36}$ 1 mark

4.  a) $\dfrac{5}{7} = \dfrac{15}{21}$ and $\dfrac{2}{3} = \dfrac{14}{21}$, so $\dfrac{5}{7} > \dfrac{2}{3}$
    b) $\dfrac{4}{5} = \dfrac{36}{45}$ and $\dfrac{7}{9} = \dfrac{35}{45}$, so $\dfrac{4}{5} > \dfrac{7}{9}$
    c) $\dfrac{3}{10} = \dfrac{21}{70}$ and $\dfrac{2}{7} = \dfrac{20}{70}$, so $\dfrac{3}{10} > \dfrac{2}{7}$
    d) $\dfrac{7}{12} = \dfrac{35}{60}$ and $\dfrac{3}{5} = \dfrac{36}{60}$, so $\dfrac{7}{12} < \dfrac{3}{5}$
    1 mark for each correct answer

5.  a) $\phantom{0}5453$
    $\times\phantom{000}14$
    $\overline{\phantom{0}21{,}8{,}1{,}2}$
    $54530$
    $\overline{76342}$
    $\phantom{0000}1$
    
    b) $\phantom{0}3561$
    $\times\phantom{000}35$
    $\overline{\phantom{0}17{,}2{,}8{,}05}$
    $10{,}6{,}830$
    $\overline{124635}$
    $\phantom{000}1\,1$
    
    1 mark for each correct answer

6.  a) 22)9027 = 41 r 5   b) 31)8427 = 27 r 10
    1 mark for each correct answer

7.  a)  8 2 3 1 5 1
        − 7 1 4 2
        8 1 6 0 0 9
    
    b)  7 5 3 1 7 2
        − 6 3 4 7 1 4
        1 1 8 4 5 8
    1 mark for each correct answer

### Workout 12 — pages 24-25

1.  a) **5400**   b) **310**
    c) **1200**   d) **2100**
    2 marks for all four correct,
    otherwise 1 mark for at least two correct

2.  a) **16**  b) **64**  c) **1**  d) **125**
    2 marks for all four correct,
    otherwise 1 mark for at least two correct

3.  a) 13)2876 = **221 r 3**   b) 12)4958 = **413 r 2**
    1 mark for each correct answer

4.  $\frac{7}{5}$   $\frac{11}{8}$   $\frac{27}{20}$   $\frac{13}{10}$
    2 marks for all four correct, otherwise
    1 mark for three in the correct order

5.  a) **6 000 000**  1 mark
    b) **2 800 000**  1 mark

6.  a) $\frac{7}{48} + \frac{5}{6} = \frac{7}{48} + \frac{40}{48} = \frac{47}{48}$  1 mark
    b) $\frac{4}{5} - \frac{2}{45} = \frac{36}{45} - \frac{2}{45} = \frac{34}{45}$  1 mark

7.  a) 4 367 106 > 4 367 016  1 mark
    b) 9 143 722 < 9 145 341  1 mark

8.  a)     6 1 0 8
         ×    7 1
           6 1 0 8
         4 2 7 5 6 0
         4 3 3 6 6 8
    
    b)     7 3 2 3
         ×    2 3
         2 1 9 6 9
         1 4 6 4 6 0
         1 6 8 4 2 9
    1 mark for each correct answer

## Spring Term

### Workout 1 — pages 26-27

1.  a) **69 000**   b) **7200**
    c) **500**      d) **9000**
    2 marks for all four correct,
    otherwise 1 mark for at least two correct

2.  a) **18 595**   b) **9823**
    c) **34 392**   d) **3591**
    2 marks for all four correct,
    otherwise 1 mark for at least two correct

3.  a) $\frac{7}{12}$  1 mark   b) $\frac{7}{18}$  1 mark

4.  a) **5 460 000**  1 mark
    b) **3 000 000**  1 mark

5.  a) **9**  1 mark    b) **−3**  1 mark
    c) **−12**  1 mark  d) **24**  1 mark

6.  **7 198 237 > 7 197 329** and
    **5 896 565 < 6 103 823** should be ticked
    1 mark for each correct answer

7.  a) $\frac{17}{21}$  1 mark   b) $\frac{7}{15}$  1 mark

### Workout 2 — pages 28-29

1.  a) **50**  b) **46**  c) **88**  d) **9**
    2 marks for all four correct,
    otherwise 1 mark for at least two correct

2.  a) **6438**  b) **7946**  c) **1558**  d) **3456**
    2 marks for all four correct,
    otherwise 1 mark for at least two correct

3.  a)       1 4
         25)3 5 0
           − 2 5
             1 0 0
           − 1 0 0
                 0
    
    b)       3 4
         12)4 0 8
           − 3 6
               4 8
             − 4 8
                 0
    1 mark for each correct answer

4.  a) $\frac{6}{5} = \frac{18}{15}$ and $\frac{4}{3} = \frac{20}{15}$, so $\frac{6}{5} < \frac{4}{3}$
    b) $\frac{7}{4} = \frac{42}{24}$ and $\frac{8}{6} = \frac{32}{24}$, so $\frac{7}{4} > \frac{8}{6}$
    1 mark for each correct answer

5.  a) **1000**  1 mark   b) **203**  1 mark
    c) **100**  1 mark    d) **7400**  1 mark

6.  a) $\frac{7}{9}$  1 mark   b) $\frac{3}{5}$  1 mark

7.  a)       2 6
         31)8 0 6
           − 6 2
             1 8 6
           − 1 8 6
                 0
    
    b)       3 3
         28)9 2 4
           − 8 4
               8 4
             − 8 4
                 0
    1 mark for each correct answer using
    any method of long division

Answers

## Workout 3 — pages 30-31

1. a) **82 200**    b) **7200**
   c) **9000**    d) **900**
   2 marks for all four correct,
   otherwise 1 mark for at least two correct

2. a) **2.3**   b) **3550**   c) **0.048**   d) **0.096**
   2 marks for all four correct,
   otherwise 1 mark for at least two correct

3. a) $4\frac{1}{4}$   1 mark    b) $3\frac{7}{9}$   1 mark

4. a) **4.2**   1 mark    b) **10.4**   1 mark

5. $\frac{2}{7}$   $\frac{2}{3}$   $\frac{5}{7}$   $\frac{31}{42}$
   2 marks for all four correct, otherwise
   1 mark for three in the correct order

6. a)
   ```
         5 0 3 3
   ×        3 1
   ─────────────
         5 0 3 3
     1 5 0 9 9 0
   ─────────────
     1 5 6 0 2 3
           1 1
   ```
   b)
   ```
         1 3 6 2
   ×        5 5
   ─────────────
     6,8,3,1 0
     6,8,3,1 0 0
   ─────────────
     7 4 9 1 0
           1
   ```
   1 mark for each correct answer

7. a) **6.5**   1 mark    b) **10.2**   1 mark

8. a) $1\frac{7}{10}$   1 mark    b) $3\frac{17}{30}$   1 mark

## Workout 4 — pages 32-33

1. a) **34.1**   b) **168.9**   c) **7200**   d) **310**
   2 marks for all four correct,
   otherwise 1 mark for at least two correct

2. a) **7058**   b) **3789**   c) **9491**   d) **1127**
   2 marks for all four correct,
   otherwise 1 mark for at least two correct

3. a)
   ```
              1 3 5
       16 ) 2 1 6 0
          - 1 6
          ─────
              5 6
           - 4 8
             ───
              8 0
            - 8 0
              ───
                0
   ```
   b)
   ```
              3 2 2
       22 ) 7 0 8 4
          - 6 6
          ─────
              4 8
           - 4 4
             ───
              4 4
            - 4 4
              ───
                0
   ```
   1 mark for each correct answer

4. a) **12**   1 mark    b) **9**   1 mark

5. E.g. $\frac{2}{5} = \frac{16}{40}$ and $\frac{3}{8} = \frac{15}{40}$
   1 mark for each correct answer

6. a) **24**   1 mark    b) **−38**   1 mark
   c) **19**   1 mark    d) **33**   1 mark

7. a)
   ```
              2 1 4
       31 ) 6 6 3 4
          - 6 2
          ─────
              4 3
           - 3 1
             ───
            1 2 4
          - 1 2 4
          ─────
                0
   ```
   b)
   ```
              1 3 5
       54 ) 7 2 9 0
          - 5 4
          ─────
            1 8 9
          - 1 6 2
          ─────
            2 7 0
          - 2 7 0
          ─────
                0
   ```
   1 mark for each correct answer

## Workout 5 — pages 34-35

1. a) **46**   b) **85**   c) **52**   d) **95**
   2 marks for all four correct,
   otherwise 1 mark for at least two correct

2. a) **48 000**    b) **1020**
   c) **12 000**    d) **600**
   2 marks for all four correct,
   otherwise 1 mark for at least two correct

3. a) $\frac{1}{6}$   1 mark    b) $\frac{1}{20}$   1 mark

4. a) **6.21**   1 mark    b) **7.92**   1 mark

5. $\frac{15}{8}$   $\frac{7}{4}$   $\frac{65}{48}$   $\frac{11}{12}$
   2 marks for all four correct, otherwise
   1 mark for three in the correct order

6. a) **6**   1 mark    b) **6**   1 mark
   c) **63**   1 mark    d) **10**   1 mark

7. a) $\frac{4}{15}$   1 mark    b) $\frac{5}{24}$   1 mark

## Workout 6 — pages 36-37

1. a) **5530**   b) **81.8**   c) **0.491**   d) **0.076**
   2 marks for all four correct,
   otherwise 1 mark for at least two correct

2. a) **2485**   b) **7110**   c) **8004**   d) **1279**
   2 marks for all four correct,
   otherwise 1 mark for at least two correct

3. a)
   ```
            3 2 r 6
       14 ) 4 5 4
          - 4 2
          ─────
              3 4
           - 2 8
             ───
                6
   ```
   b)
   ```
           2 5 r 14
       23 ) 5 8 9
          - 4 6
          ─────
            1 2 9
          - 1 1 5
          ─────
              1 4
   ```
   1 mark for each correct answer

4. a) $\frac{1}{6}$   1 mark    b) $\frac{3}{20}$   1 mark

5. a) $\frac{16}{28}$   1 mark    b) $\frac{24}{42}$   1 mark

6.  a) $8 \times 7 = 56$ so $0.8 \times 7 = $ **5.6**  1 mark
    b) $51 \times 4 = 204$ so $5.1 \times 4 = $ **20.4**  1 mark
    c) $29 \times 3 = 87$ so $2.9 \times 3 = $ **8.7**  1 mark
    d) $11 \times 21 = 231$ so $1.1 \times 21 = $ **23.1**  1 mark

7.  a) $\frac{3}{8} + \frac{1}{3} = \frac{9}{24} + \frac{8}{24} = \frac{17}{24}$  1 mark
    b) $\frac{5}{6} - \frac{2}{5} = \frac{25}{30} - \frac{12}{30} = \frac{13}{30}$  1 mark

## Workout 7 — pages 38-39

1.  a) **13 200**   b) **32 000**
    c) **12 000**   d) **40**
    2 marks for all four correct,
    otherwise 1 mark for at least two correct

2.  a) **1000** 1 mark   b) **10** 1 mark
    c) **100** 1 mark    d) **10** 1 mark

3.  a) $\frac{1}{6}$  1 mark   b) $\frac{1}{20}$  1 mark

4.  a) **2 000 000**  1 mark
    b) **630 000**  1 mark

5.  $\frac{53}{40}$   $\frac{7}{5}$   $\frac{31}{20}$   $\frac{17}{10}$
    2 marks for all four correct, otherwise
    1 mark for three in the correct order

6.  $18\,000 \div 900 > 1800 \div 9$ is **false**  1 mark
    $200 \times 600 < 20\,000 \times 60$ is **true**  1 mark

7.  a) $\frac{3}{10}$  1 mark   b) $\frac{3}{35}$  1 mark

## Workout 8 — pages 40-41

1.  a) **41**   b) **3**   c) **39**   d) **119**
    2 marks for all four correct,
    otherwise 1 mark for at least two correct

2.  a) **6000**   b) **48 000**
    c) **10 800**   d) **770**
    2 marks for all four correct,
    otherwise 1 mark for at least two correct

3.  a)  $\phantom{8|}$**0.1 2 5**   b) $\phantom{8|}$**0.6 2 5**
        $8\overline{|1.^10^20^40}$       $8\overline{|5.^50^20^40}$
    1 mark for each correct answer

4.  a) $\frac{11}{7} = \frac{33}{21}$, so $\frac{11}{7} < \frac{35}{21}$  1 mark
    b) $\frac{13}{8} = \frac{52}{32}$, so $\frac{42}{32} < \frac{13}{8}$  1 mark

5.  a) $341 \times 4 = 1364$ so $3.41 \times 4 = $ **13.64**
    b) $408 \times 5 = 2040$ so $4.08 \times 5 = $ **20.4**
    1 mark for each correct answer. You can use
    column multiplication for the first step.

6.  a) **9** 1 mark   b) **60** 1 mark
    c) **7** 1 mark   d) **21** 1 mark

7.  a) $1\frac{9}{20}$  1 mark   b) $7\frac{13}{21}$  1 mark

## Workout 9 — pages 42-43

1.  a) **843** 1 mark   b) **270** 1 mark
    c) **0.066** 1 mark   d) **0.081** 1 mark

2.  a) **4346**   b) **4693**   c) **9202**   d) **652**
    2 marks for all four correct,
    otherwise 1 mark for at least two correct

3.  a)  $\phantom{7|}$**2.4**   b) $\phantom{6|}$**3.9**
        $7\overline{|1^16.^28}$       $6\overline{|2^23.^54}$
    1 mark for each correct answer

4.  $\frac{18}{30}$ and $\frac{27}{45}$ should be circled.
    1 mark for each correct answer.
    Lose a mark for an incorrect answer.

5.  a) $\phantom{xx}$ 2 2 3   b) $\phantom{xx}$ 4 3 0 9
       $\times \phantom{xx}$ 8 4      $\times \phantom{xxx}$ 5 9
       $\phantom{xx}$ 8 9 $_1$2       $\phantom{x}$ 3 8 $_2$7 8 $_8$1
       1 7 $_1$8 4 0                  2 1 $_5$4 $_4$5 0
       1 8 7 3 2                      2 5 4 2 3 1
       $\phantom{xx}$ 1 1             $\phantom{xx}$ 1 1 1
    1 mark for each correct answer

6.  a) $\frac{1}{5} \times \frac{3}{4} = \frac{3}{20}$  1 mark
    b) $\frac{3}{8} \times \frac{3}{7} = \frac{9}{56}$  1 mark

7.  a) $\phantom{3|}$**1 4.9**   b) $\phantom{7|}$**1 2.8**
       $3\overline{|4^14.^27}$       $7\overline{|8^19.^56}$
    1 mark for each correct answer

## Workout 10 — pages 44-45

1.  a) **59**   b) **95**   c) **49**   d) **122**
    2 marks for all four correct,
    otherwise 1 mark for at least two correct

2.  a) **2001** 1 mark   b) **1999** 1 mark
    c) **3999** 1 mark   d) **5009** 1 mark

3.  a) $\phantom{12|}$**1 3 5 r 6**   b) $\phantom{25|}$**2 3 1 r 5**
       $12\overline{|1\ 6\ 2\ 6}$        $25\overline{|5\ 7\ 8\ 0}$
       $-1\ 2$                           $-5\ 0$
       $\phantom{-}\ \ 4\ 2$             $\phantom{-}\ \ 7\ 8$
       $\phantom{-}-3\ 6$                $\phantom{-}-7\ 5$
       $\phantom{-x}\ \ 6\ 6$            $\phantom{-x}\ \ 3\ 0$
       $\phantom{-x}-6\ 0$               $\phantom{-x}-2\ 5$
       $\phantom{-xxx}\ 6$               $\phantom{-xxx}\ 5$
    1 mark for each correct answer

Answers

4.  a) **1.57**    b) **3.64**
       5)7.²8³5        8)2²9.⁵1³2
    1 mark for each correct answer

5.  a) $\frac{2}{15}$  1 mark    b) $\frac{3}{28}$  1 mark

6.  $\frac{11}{6}$    $\frac{21}{12}$    $\frac{5}{3}$    $\frac{13}{8}$
    2 marks for all four correct, otherwise
    1 mark for three in the correct order

7.  a) $\frac{1}{2}$  1 mark    b) $\frac{1}{6}$  1 mark

## Workout 11 — pages 46-47

1.  a) **2**   b) **68**   c) **18**   d) **10**
    2 marks for all four correct,
    otherwise 1 mark for at least two correct

2.  a) **300**   b) **4200**   c) **1100**   d) **16 000**
    2 marks for all four correct,
    otherwise 1 mark for at least two correct

3.  a) **35%**  1 mark    b) **66%**  1 mark
    c) **92%**  1 mark    d) **48%**  1 mark

4.  a) **5 770 000**    b) **810 000**
    1 mark for each correct answer

5.  a) 132 × 7 = 924 so 1.32 × 7 = **9.24**
    b) 13 × 31 = 403 so 13 × 3.1 = **40.3**
    1 mark for each correct answer. You can use column multiplication for the first step.

6.  **45% = $\frac{9}{20}$** and **98% = 0.98** should be ticked
    1 mark for each correct answer.
    Lose a mark for an incorrect answer.

7.  a)       **224 r 5**    b)       **201 r 9**
       35)7 8 4 5              23)4 6 3 2
         − 7 0                   − 4 6
           8 4                     0 3 2
         − 7 0                   − 2 3
           1 4 5                       9
         − 1 4 0
               5
    1 mark for each correct answer

## Workout 12 — pages 48-49

1.  a) **12 586**    b) **5262**
    c) **21 335**    d) **5911**
    2 marks for all four correct,
    otherwise 1 mark for at least two correct

2.  a) **12**   b) **72**   c) **0**   d) **18**
    2 marks for all four correct,
    otherwise 1 mark for at least two correct

3.  a) **5**  1 mark    b) **9**  1 mark
    c) **36**  1 mark   d) **48**  1 mark

4.  a) $4\frac{5}{24}$  1 mark    b) $2\frac{7}{18}$  1 mark

5.  a)       **5.8**       b)       **4.84**
       4)2²3.³2               9)4⁴3.⁷5³6
    1 mark for each correct answer

6.  a) 10% = **8**      b) 10% = **12**
       5% = **4**          60% = **72**
       15% = **12**        5% = **6**
                           65% = **78**
    1 mark for each correct answer

7.  a)    **0.375**       b)    **0.875**
       8)3.³0⁶0⁴0           8)7.⁷0⁶0⁴0
    1 mark for each correct answer

## Summer Term

### Workout 1 — pages 50-51

1.  a) **53.165**    b) **85.3**
    c) **246.57**    d) **54.046**
    2 marks for all four correct,
    otherwise 1 mark for at least two correct

2.  a) $\frac{1}{12}$  1 mark    b) $\frac{5}{42}$  1 mark

3.  a) **−17**  1 mark    b) **−18**  1 mark
    c) **15**  1 mark     d) **16**  1 mark

4.  **1 546 464**, **1 546 465**, **1 546 564**, **1 556 464**
    2 marks for all four correct, otherwise
    1 mark for three in the correct order

5.  a) **2**   b) **2.4**   c) **1.8**   d) **2.8**
    2 marks for all four correct, otherwise
    1 mark for at least two correct

6.  a) $\frac{3}{16}$  1 mark    b) $\frac{13}{24}$  1 mark

7.  a)       **256**        b)       **225**
       14)3 5 8 4              25)5 6 2 5
         − 2 8                   − 5 0
           7 8                     6 2
         − 7 0                   − 5 0
           8 4                     1 2 5
         − 8 4                   − 1 2 5
             0                         0
    1 mark for each correct answer

## Workout 2 — pages 52-53

1. a) **6616**  b) **5465**  c) **6645**  d) **7326**
   2 marks for all four correct, otherwise
   1 mark for at least two correct

2. −11  −7  **−3**  **1**  **5**
   1 mark for all three correct

3. a) $\frac{1}{10}$  1 mark   b) $\frac{1}{18}$  1 mark

4. $\frac{4}{5} = \frac{16}{20} = \frac{36}{45}$  1 mark

5. a) 
   ```
         5 6 r 7
   11 | 6 2 3
       − 5 5
         7 3
       − 6 6
           7
   ```
   b)
   ```
         7 5 r 6
   12 | 9 0 6
       − 8 4
         6 6
       − 6 0
           6
   ```
   1 mark for each correct answer

6. a) 8 ÷ 2 − 4 = 4 − 4 = **0**  1 mark
   b) 5 + 2 × 3 = 5 + 6 = **11**  1 mark
   c) 14 + 8 ÷ 4 = 14 + 2 = **16**  1 mark

7. a) $\frac{1}{7} + \frac{3}{4} = \frac{4}{28} + \frac{21}{28} = \frac{25}{28}$  1 mark
   b) $\frac{2}{5} + \frac{1}{6} = \frac{12}{30} + \frac{5}{30} = \frac{17}{30}$  1 mark

8. a) **21**  b) **420**  c) **437**
   1 mark for each correct answer

## Workout 3 — pages 54-55

1. a) $\frac{1}{5}$  1 mark   b) $\frac{1}{3}$  1 mark

2. a) **0.66**  1 mark   b) **0.72**  1 mark

3. a) **1278**  b) **4413**  c) **2319**
   1 mark for each correct answer

4. 11  5  **−1**  **−7**  **−13**
   2 marks for all three correct,
   otherwise 1 mark for two correct

5. a)
   ```
       4 1 9
   ×    1 6
     2 5₁5₄4
     4 1 9 0
     6 7 0 4
         1
   ```
   b)
   ```
       2 5 3
   ×    3 2
       5 0 6
     7₁5 9 0
     8 0 9 6
         1
   ```
   1 mark for each correct answer

6. a) $\frac{3}{20}$ = 0.**15** = **15%**  1 mark
   b) $\frac{3}{8}$ = 0.375 = **37.5%**  1 mark
   c) $\frac{41}{50}$ = 0.82 = **82%**  1 mark

7. a) 
   ```
       2.25
   4 | 9.¹0²0
   ```
   b)
   ```
       2.4
   5 | 1¹2.⁰0
   ```
   1 mark for each correct answer

## Workout 4 — pages 56-57

1. **466 123**, **464 123**, **446 234**, **446 123**
   1 mark for all correct

2. a) 0.06 × 7 = **0.42**   b) 0.06 × **6** = 0.36
   c) 0.09 × **5** = 0.45   d) **0.08** × 5 = 0.4
   2 marks for all four correct, otherwise
   1 mark for three in the correct order

3. a) $\frac{20}{3}$  b) $\frac{5}{4}$  c) $\frac{7}{4}$
   1 mark for each correct answer

4. a)
   ```
         2 4 5 7
   ×       3 4
       9,8,2,2 8
     7,3,7,2 1 0
     8 3 5 3 8
         1 1
   ```
   b)
   ```
         8 7 0 4
   ×       2 6
       5 2,2 2,2 4
     1 7,4 0 8 0
     2 2 6 3 0 4
         1   1
   ```
   1 mark for each correct answer

5. $\frac{31}{36}$  $\frac{8}{9}$  ☐$\frac{5}{6}$  ◯$\frac{17}{18}$
   1 mark for each correct answer

6. a) $3\frac{1}{2} + \frac{3}{4} = \frac{7}{2} + \frac{3}{4} = \frac{14}{4} + \frac{3}{4} = \frac{17}{4}$
   b) $4\frac{1}{6} + \frac{5}{3} = \frac{25}{6} + \frac{10}{6} = \frac{35}{6}$
   1 mark for each correct answer

7. a) $\frac{23}{25} = \frac{92}{100} = 0.92 > 0.91$
   b) $\frac{17}{20} = \frac{85}{100} = 0.85 = 85\% < 86\%$
   1 mark for each correct answer

## Workout 5 — pages 58-59

1. a) $1\frac{5}{6} = \frac{11}{6}$, so $\frac{11}{6} < \frac{13}{6}$
   b) $1\frac{2}{3} = \frac{5}{3}$, so $\frac{5}{3} > \frac{4}{3}$
   1 mark for both correct

2. a) **5**  1 mark   b) **−13**  1 mark
   c) **17**  1 mark   d) **−32**  1 mark

3. a) $\frac{7}{6}$  1 mark   b) $\frac{3}{2}$  1 mark

4. $\frac{51}{100}$   $\frac{27}{50}$   $\frac{57}{100}$   $\frac{3}{5}$   $\frac{63}{100}$
   1 mark for each correct answer

5. a) $6 + 5 \times 8 + 2 = 6 + 40 + 2 = \mathbf{48}$
   b) $(6 + 5) \times 8 + 2 = 11 \times 8 + 2 = 88 + 2 = \mathbf{90}$
   c) $(6 + 5) \times (8 + 2) = 11 \times 10 = \mathbf{110}$
   1 mark for each correct answer

6. a)
   ```
        54
   13 ) 702
       -65
        52
       -52
         0
   ```
   b)
   ```
        69
   24 ) 1656
       -144
        216
       -216
          0
   ```
   1 mark for each correct answer

7. a) $\frac{6}{7} + \frac{4}{21} = \frac{18}{21} + \frac{4}{21} = \mathbf{\frac{22}{21}}$
   b) $\frac{4}{5} + \frac{1}{2} = \frac{8}{10} + \frac{5}{10} = \mathbf{\frac{13}{10}}$
   1 mark for each correct answer

## Workout 6 — pages 60-61

1. a) **0.6**   b) **2.5**   c) **360**   d) **42**
   2 marks for all four correct, otherwise 1 mark for at least two correct

2. a) **0.007**   b) **0.109**   c) **0.38**
   d) **0.162**   e) **0.269**   f) **1.503**
   3 marks for all six correct, otherwise
   2 marks for at least four correct, or
   1 mark for at least two correct

3. a) $\mathbf{0.625} = \frac{5}{8} = \mathbf{62.5\%}$   1 mark
   b) $\mathbf{52\%} = 0.52 = \mathbf{\frac{13}{25}}$   1 mark

4. a) **1220** 1 mark   b) **403** 1 mark
   c) **204** 1 mark   d) **1009** 1 mark

5. a) **−8**   b) **−9**
   1 mark for both correct

6. a)
   ```
        40.6
   5 ) 2²03.³0
   ```
   b)
   ```
        123.8
   5 ) 6¹1⁴9.⁴0
   ```
   1 mark for each correct answer

7. a) $\frac{5}{8} \times \frac{2}{5} = \frac{10}{40} = \mathbf{\frac{1}{4}}$   1 mark
   b) $\frac{4}{7} \times \frac{3}{8} = \frac{12}{56} = \mathbf{\frac{3}{14}}$   1 mark

## Workout 7 — pages 62-63

1. a) **8751**   b) **9649**   c) **6537**   d) **952**
   2 marks for all four correct,
   otherwise 1 mark for at least two correct

2. a) **135**   b) **100.6**   c) **512**   d) **9020**
   2 marks for all four correct,
   otherwise 1 mark for at least two correct

3. a) $\frac{5}{7}$   b) $\frac{3}{8}$   c) $\frac{3}{5}$
   1 mark for each correct answer

4. $\frac{45}{50}$   $\frac{19}{20}$   $\boxed{\frac{18}{40}}$   $\frac{5}{8}$
   1 mark for the correct fraction circled

5. a) **10**   b) **44**   c) **117**   d) **84**
   1 mark for each correct answer

6. $\frac{3}{4}$   $\frac{19}{28}$   $\frac{9}{14}$   $\frac{4}{7}$
   2 marks for all four correct, otherwise
   1 mark for three in the correct order

7. a)
   ```
          205 r 20
   24 ) 4940
       -48
        140
       -120
         20
   ```
   b)
   ```
          367 r 5
   15 ) 5510
       -45
        101
        -90
        110
       -105
          5
   ```
   1 mark for each correct answer

## Workout 8 — pages 64-65

1. a) **90**   b) **900**   c) **7700**   d) **18 000**
   2 marks for all four correct, otherwise
   1 mark for at least two correct

2. a) **−3** 1 mark   b) **−4** 1 mark
   c) **−8** 1 mark   d) **−16** 1 mark

3. a) **6 100 000** 1 mark   b) **91 600** 1 mark

4. a) **35%** 1 mark   b) **96%** 1 mark

5. a) $\frac{7}{12} + \frac{2}{5} = \frac{35}{60} + \frac{24}{60} = \mathbf{\frac{59}{60}}$   1 mark
   b) $\frac{8}{9} + \frac{5}{6} = \frac{16}{18} + \frac{15}{18} = \mathbf{\frac{31}{18}}$   1 mark

6. a)
   ```
         931
   ×      22
        1862
       18620
       20482
         1 1
   ```
   b)
   ```
        1362
   ×      55
        6₈3₁10
       6₈3₁100
       74910
          1
   ```
   1 mark for each correct answer

7. a) $\mathbf{\frac{9}{4}}$ 1 mark   b) $\mathbf{\frac{10}{3}}$ 1 mark

## Workout 9 — pages 66-67

1. a) **3814**   b) **4395**   c) **8460**   d) **8137**
   2 marks for all four correct, otherwise
   1 mark for at least two correct

2. a) **0.125** 1 mark b) **0.875** 1 mark
3. a) **11** 1 mark b) **−11** 1 mark
   c) **−15** 1 mark d) **20** 1 mark
4. a) $8 + 6 \div 3 - 7 = 8 + 2 - 7 = \mathbf{3}$
   b) $2 \times (5 + 7) \div 4 = 2 \times 12 \div 4 = 24 \div 4 = \mathbf{6}$
   1 mark for each correct answer
5. a) $\frac{1}{11} + \frac{3}{5} = \frac{5}{55} + \frac{33}{55} = \mathbf{\frac{38}{55}}$ 1 mark
   b) $\frac{7}{12} + \frac{2}{9} = \frac{21}{36} + \frac{8}{36} = \mathbf{\frac{29}{36}}$ 1 mark
6. a) **12.75**
      $4\overline{)51^13^20}$
   b) **2.35**
      $20\overline{)4\,47.^70^{10}0}$
   1 mark for each correct answer
7. a) $\frac{7}{9} \times \frac{3}{5} = \frac{21}{45} = \mathbf{\frac{7}{15}}$ 1 mark
   b) $\frac{5}{12} \times \frac{4}{7} = \frac{20}{84} = \mathbf{\frac{5}{21}}$ 1 mark

## Workout 10 — pages 68-69

1. a) **0.093** b) **0.361** c) **18.2** d) **2.014**
   2 marks for all four correct, otherwise
   1 mark for at least two correct
2. a) **2100** 1 mark b) **4500** 1 mark
   c) **1461** 1 mark d) **4138** 1 mark
3. $\frac{2}{3}$  [$\frac{5}{8}$]  ($\frac{5}{6}$)  $\frac{3}{4}$
   1 mark for each correct answer
4. a) $\frac{5}{8}$ 1 mark b) $\frac{2}{3}$ 1 mark
5. a) **17.2** 1 mark b) **6.6** 1 mark
6. a) $\frac{6}{7} \times \frac{2}{3} = \frac{12}{21} = \mathbf{\frac{4}{7}}$ 1 mark
   b) $\frac{15}{22} \times \frac{4}{5} = \frac{60}{110} = \mathbf{\frac{6}{11}}$ 1 mark
7. a) **409 r 6**
      $21\overline{)8595}$
      $-84$
      $\phantom{0}195$
      $-189$
      $\phantom{00}6$
   b) **249 r 1**
      $31\overline{)7720}$
      $-62$
      $\phantom{0}152$
      $-124$
      $\phantom{00}280$
      $-279$
      $\phantom{000}1$
   1 mark for each correct answer

## Workout 11 — pages 70-71

1. a) **505** 1 mark b) **2211** 1 mark
   c) **801** 1 mark d) **102** 1 mark
2. a) $\frac{7}{10}$ 1 mark b) $\frac{3}{20}$ 1 mark
3. a) $\frac{10}{9} = \frac{40}{36}, \frac{10}{9} < \frac{41}{36}$ 1 mark
   b) $\frac{8}{7} = \frac{56}{49}$, so $\frac{55}{49} < \frac{8}{7}$ 1 mark
4. $(14 - 5) \times 2^2 = 9 \times 2^2 = 9 \times 4 = \mathbf{36}$ 1 mark
5. a) **90** b) **1120** c) **1275**
   1 mark for each correct answer
6. a) $\frac{12}{25} = 0.48 = \mathbf{48\%}$ 1 mark
   b) $\frac{7}{8} = 0.875 = \mathbf{87.5\%}$ 1 mark
7. a)  $\phantom{00}223$
       $\times\phantom{00}84$
       $\phantom{0}\overline{\phantom{00}892}$
       $\phantom{0}17{,}840$
       $\phantom{0}\overline{18732}$
       $\phantom{000}{}_1\,{}_1$
   b)  $\phantom{00}4309$
       $\times\phantom{000}59$
       $\phantom{0}\overline{38{,}781}$
       $215{,}450$
       $\overline{254231}$
       $\phantom{00}{}_1\,{}_1\,{}_1$
   1 mark for each correct answer

## Workout 12 — pages 72-73

1. a) **3.5** b) **2.7** c) **2.4** d) **0.55**
   2 marks for all four correct, otherwise 1 mark
   for at least two correct
2. a) **3** 1 mark b) **8** 1 mark
   c) **2** 1 mark d) **20** 1 mark
3. a) $\frac{39}{44}$ 1 mark b) $\frac{2}{63}$ 1 mark
4. a) **56.08** 1 mark b) **2.45** 1 mark
5. a) $3 + (9 - 5) \times 12 = 3 + 4 \times 12 = 3 + 48 = \mathbf{51}$
   b) $10 - 3 + 8 \div 2 = 10 - 3 + 4 = \mathbf{11}$
   1 mark for each correct answer
6. a)  **54**
      $13\overline{)702}$
      $-65$
      $\phantom{0}\overline{52}$
      $-52$
      $\phantom{00}\overline{0}$
   b)  **622 r 2**
      $16\overline{)9954}$
      $-96$
      $\phantom{0}\overline{35}$
      $-32$
      $\phantom{0}\overline{34}$
      $-32$
      $\phantom{00}\overline{2}$
   1 mark for each correct answer
7. a) $\frac{1}{14}$ 1 mark b) $\frac{3}{17}$ 1 mark

## Puzzle: Fractional Footpaths — page 74

Shortest route = 1.426 miles
Longest route = 1.595 miles

Answers